THE COMPLETE BOOK OF
BUSINESS
ETIQUETTE

THE COMPLETE BOOK OF
BUSINESS
ETIQUETTE

LYNNE BRENNAN
& DAVID BLOCK

PIATKUS

In general, the masculine forms of pronouns and nouns are used throughout this book, for the sake of brevity.

Copyright © 1991 Lynne Brennan and David Block

First published in 1991 by
Judy Piatkus (Publishers) LImited
5 Windmill Street, London W1P 1HF

First paperback edition 1992

Reprinted 1996

British Library Cataloguing in Publication Data
Brennan, Lynne
  The complete book of business etiquette.
  I. Title   II. Block, David
  658.3

    ISBN 0–7499–1052–6
    ISBN 0–7499–1148–4 (pbk)

Designed by Paul Saunders
Cartoons by Dave Smee
Typeset by Phoenix Photosetting, Chatham, Kent
Printed and bound in Great Britain by
Biddles Ltd, Guildford and King's Lynn

From David: To Ruth and Lucia, precious people.

From Lynne: For all the people who have believed in me – especially Kevin, Sarah, Karen, Nicola, Irene and Arthur.

ACKNOWLEDGEMENTS

Very special thanks to David Block for putting my thoughts into words and for his creative contributions and support.

For help, support and encouragement many thanks to Derek and Silvie Cooke, Des and Vera Howard, Aldo and Tina Breda, Gill Haworth and Pam Burchfield. Also everyone at Piatkus but especially Heather Rocklin, Gill Cormode, Judy Piatkus, Philip Cotterell and Jana Sommerlad. Thanks also to Mike Cox of National Westminster Bank plc, and Jim Smith and Jonathon van der Borgh.

Sincere thanks to Malcolm Hamer for introducing us to Piatkus and for his professional skills; Gayle Colman for endless hours of research; Lucia Block and Sarah Brennan for their contributions to the research and early proof reading.

Thanks also to everyone who has supplied quotes and anyone else who has participated knowingly or unknowingly in the production of this book.

Lynne Brennan

CONTENTS

Part II SOCIAL SKILLS

Part III FOREIGN ETIQUETTE

INTRODUCTION

THE practice of good business etiquette generates immediate benefits. It enhances customer and staff relationships. It helps executives handle themselves effectively and confidently in every kind of
social and interactive situation. It improves the quality of working life
for everyone in a company. And it adds value to every other area of company life – from production through marketing and selling, sales promotion, training and personnel development to customer service.

Those who behave wrongly are not necessarily discourteous or rude;
usually they are simply oblivious of their gaffes. But that very oblivion
brands them as lacking polish, social education and perhaps respect for
others. As such, their progress along the path to material and career
success is impaired, as is the contribution they make on behalf of their
company.

The Complete Book of Business Etiquette starts by suggesting how to
make the best possible impression through dress, behaviour and attitude at a job interview, and then how to maintain that impression in the
job. We offer solid information on every area of communications, from
face-to-face to electronically assisted. There is guidance on how to
criticise with positive results and how to turn complaints into sales. We
show how good working relationships can be established and, accepting
that business people are also flesh and blood, on avoiding dangerous
ones.

There is advice on how to win at meetings without the others feeling
they've lost, and we cover such tricky topics as controlling rumour and
gossip without getting one's fingers burnt. The book demonstrates how
to deal with difficult situations, awkward customers and almost impossible clients and colleagues. It does not even stop short at what to do
when your own body conspires against you in company!

The Complete Book of Business Etiquette takes you to receptions, lunch and dinner, and arms you with the necessary knowledge to take you to the opera or to Ascot and social stops along the way.

If you are a woman in business, or one of the many thousands returning to it, the book will help give you the confidence (if you need it) to keep up with and overtake the men – and without them resenting it. For men it demonstrates, among other things, how not to feel threatened or baffled by women in business.

And finally: export or die of embarrassment – how to win over foreign customers before they win over you. Essential advice is offered on the human skills involved in doing business in two of the world's most important overseas markets: Japan and the Middle East. It would be impossible to list the different forms of etiquette in all the world's business centres, so we have concentrated on the two where behaviour is a cardinal factor in the conduct of business.

Behaving correctly is, however, still only part of the story. We can learn a lot from following accepted rules and codes. But the basis of true etiquette is respect: for others and for oneself. From the moment the business day starts, millions of us change our nature, switching from our family and private personalities into what we consider to be the appropriate attitudes and postures of our profession. By assuming the roles of banker, industrialist, engineer, marketing and sales person, lawyer, writer and so on, many of us part company with our real selves. The acting out of these synthetic personalities, day in and day out, does not lead to long-term fulfilment; it is more likely to result in disillusionment, disappointment and, at worst, psychological malaise. But by following a code of behaviour based on respecting others as unique individuals we will create a far more honest, healthy and enjoyable business life for ourselves and our colleagues. And in so doing, we will add enormously to our effectiveness as business people. How to demonstrate that respect is the purpose of this book.

As we have already stated, few people deliberately behave incorrectly. The problem stems from their lack of awareness of good business etiquette. So if you come across advice in this book which you consider to be rather obvious, please remember that it is included because someone, somewhere, doesn't think it is.

Part I

At Work

Chapter 1

THE INTERVIEW

MUTUAL respect is the keynote of any civilised job interview. But if the stakes are high, the interviewee is the one on the spot; he has to make the winning impression. With so many cards hidden, however, that can be far from straightforward. So an elegant command of business etiquette should give him a fighting chance of landing the job. This is particularly important when facing interviewers whose strong suit is incivility, whether inherent or as part of the grilling procedure. Nothing will win over such an approach more effectively than steadfast courtesy.

Selecting staff is no picnic either. But, under normal circumstances, the most effective interviewer is the one who behaves with respect to others. Apart from anything else, few people ever forget the courtesy or otherwise shown to them when they were at their most vulnerable.

Phoning for the appointment

Some job advertisements require the applicant to phone for an appointment. When you do, have your CV handy; this will save time and the answers to any detailed questions about education and past career will roll smoothly and competently off the tongue.

Nervousness can be at its height at this point, so if the interviewer takes the call, and he is good at his job, he will help the applicant by sounding welcoming and interested.

Preparation

It is a courtesy at the interview to demonstrate that it is *this* job you are after, rather than just *a* job. So it is a good idea to research a company beforehand. You can do so by asking them to send you some company literature such as their house magazine or annual report. If that's impractical, and they are a PLC, the report can be obtained from Companies House (see Useful Addresses). The effort is for your personal benefit too; you owe it to yourself to confirm that you would fit in with an organisation whose culture is expressed in these publications.

The interviewer too, being a professional, will have returned the courtesy by reading the applicant's CV in advance of the interview.

Timing

> There will always be a points failure at Sodslaw Junction or a burst water main on the Grimway By-pass. Offering these as excuses doesn't create a good impression and may signify slackness.

If, despite every effort, you are still delayed, you should phone as soon as you can to give the interviewer an estimate of your time of arrival. Explain briefly and apologise then and there; if you wait until you arrive, it will have given the interviewer lots of time to think ill of you.

Ideally, arrive fifteen to twenty minutes early. This not only gives you a chance to unwind and soak up the ambience, but if the interviewer is free he may appreciate the opportunity to get ahead.

Appearance

For most job interviews women should wear a smart business outfit (see Chapter 19). Men should wear suit, shirt and tie.

With your few minutes in hand, you've a chance to slip into the reception area toilet with pocket tissues, comb and nail file, to check that your appearance is pristine and crumb-free. A small clothes brush may be useful, too. Hands are particularly important: nails must be scrupulously clean and well manicured. Women, as a matter of course, should

> *Pre-interview checklist:*
> - Is hair neat and tidy?
> - Are hands and nails well groomed?
> - Check for loose hairs or dandruff on shoulders
> - Women should make sure tights are unladdered and unwrinkled
> - Double check that make-up/shave is perfect
> - Go to the loo

remember to bring make-up repair kit and spare tights. Shoes should be clean and polished, and men should wear socks long enough to ensure that, when seated, the lower leg is covered.

Entrance

Good-will can be accumulated even before you are called to the interview room. Being pleasant and good-mannered to everyone, from the commissionaire and receptionist onward, can create a pleasing atmosphere that will improve everyone's mood and attitude to you. As bosses sometimes ask their secretaries and others for their view of candidates, it's worth scoring a few legitimate points before you're out of the starting blocks.

The encounter

First impressions are critical. It is a statistical fact that the outcome of many interviews is decided in the opening thirty seconds. So you can rack up points instantaneously by remembering the interviewers' names. Reinforce your powers of recollection by repeating them as you are introduced – 'Good morning, Mr Jones . . . Good morning, Mr Nyakotorimochu . . .' and by keeping their business cards in front of you. Don't use their first names unless you are specifically asked to do so.

A man gives his first and last names, and does not call himself 'Mr'. 'Mr' is a courtesy title added by another person. The same is true for a woman, who should give her first and last name, without the 'Mrs' or 'Miss', unless her status is considered relevant.

In the majority of cases, communicate with the interviewer in a friendly and respectful manner, regarding them as individuals rather than just as icons along one's career path. Polite self-assurance is what you should aim for.

It all starts with the handshake. Unless the person who greets you takes the initiative, you should offer your hand first to the prospective boss, whether male or female. It is worth checking your grip: a weak and flaccid one gives a corresponding impression; nor should it be a pumping iron display. The proper handshake is firm and dry and held for just two to three seconds.

The interviewer demonstrates courtesy to the applicant by, if possible, not taking calls or allowing any other interruptions during the interview.

Body talk

Civility and openness should be communicated from the moment you sit down. Arms should be uncrossed, so you don't look defensive. To look and feel relaxed, be careful not to perch. Sit with your bottom tucked well into the back of the chair: be alert and attentive and make direct eye contact.

Remember not to allow your nerves to cause distracting gestures like swinging or contorting your legs, rummaging around your face or constantly appraising your jewellery.

> When facing an interview panel, tension often makes you lock on to a friendly and responsive face. It's worth making the effort to unclamp your gaze and share it among all the others.

Coffee talk

The simple question, 'Would you like a tea or coffee?', seems to have the same stupefying effect on some people as the tie-breaker in *Mastermind*. 'Oh . . . aren't you having one? I won't then, thanks. Sure, yes, absolutely. Oh, all right, sorry to trouble you, yes please . . . whatever's easiest . . . don't mind. I'd prefer coffee actually. Sorry. White with milk please, thanks very much indeed. . . .'

The preferred alternatives are the simple: (a) 'No thanks, I won't right now', or (b) 'Yes please, tea/coffee would be very nice.' Consider laying off the biscuits as they can be crumbly and awkward to handle and may impede coherence.

No smoking

Even if the interviewer is shrouded in fumes from his own cigarette or cigar, you shouldn't light up one of your own. There may be others in the room who disapprove, perhaps company rules restrict the practice, and anyway, why risk any negative reaction?

Nowadays even interviewers themselves should ask the permission of applicants before smoking.

. . . Or slandering

However much the interviewer may probe, don't malign your current or former employers. It's a loser's approach paying cheap and short-term dividends. Your response to such questioning should show your understanding of why a person or company operates in a particular way, without being disdainful or over-critical. Far better merely to disassociate yourself from their actions. Remember that the interviewer may briefly relish hearing others criticised, but may wonder if one day he and his company will be subject to a similar attack. Also, he may interpret your remarks in a different way – believing you were the one at fault because you couldn't get on with people or fit in.

Wherever possible, you should give some credit for your successes to those you worked with. This will demonstrate your ability to work as part of a team.

> 'In business, however good you may think you are, most people judge you only by your behaviour.'
>
> TERRY J. NASH, Director General, The Chartered Institute of Marketing.

Revelations

You don't have to give detailed answers to personal questions. If you have experienced a private tragedy that you honestly believe will *not* affect your work, it is no one's business but yours.

Where relevant, you must admit health handicaps or likely stays in hospital. If you are handicapped, you should not attempt to trivialise it, nor should you be defensive. The best approach is that your handicap motivates you to have extra drive and determination.

Objections

If something is said that you disagree with, you should politely and respectfully say so. Should the interviewer dig his heels in over a fundamental issue on which you take an opposing view, you must maintain your integrity – failure to do so is at your future peril. But be careful not to be dogmatic, and be wary of a potential employer with that tendency.

However badly you need the job, always have self-respect and never allow anyone to be rude to you without redress. At times, you may feel the urge to take a verbal counter-swing at an offensive interviewer. Instead, offer him the opportunity to withdraw the affront and to apologise. Otherwise, politely end the interview and leave.

Failure to communicate

If you are not putting yourself across adequately, there is nothing wrong – subject to time constraints – in asking for a retrial. Apologise and, with humour if possible, explain the problem, saying you would like briefly to try to restate your position.

Money

An interviewee should not broach the subject of money before all the facets of the job have been covered. In an ideal world, salary levels, increments and increases will be based on experience, expertise, net contribution and anticipated working performance. If they aren't, don't show resentment, show realism; this *isn't* an ideal world. But don't sell yourself short. If the salary is not negotiable, it may be worth enquiring about other perks, such as a car, pension and so on.

> If you are given a tour around the company, it isn't a free excursion, it's a mobile method of indicating whether you are going to fit in. Get involved by asking questions about the installations and procedures that interest you.

The exit

When the interview is clearly at an end, you should leave in the same way as you entered, regardless of how you think you got on. Smile and thank them for seeing you. If appropriate, ask when you can expect to hear from them. You should shake each interviewer's hand, say goodbye and then leave without stuttering around the doorway. Don't forget to acknowledge the reception staff as you sail out.

The follow-up

While you are waiting to hear the verdict – and whether or not you think you will get the job – it's courteous to write a short thank-you note to the chief interviewer. Subject to its untoadying tone, it will not be unappreciated, and will make you feel good too.

Chapter 2

A NEW JOB

WHEN you start a new job, your every move and mannerism is under scrutiny. Heads will swivel and faces curl round corners; expressions will be curious, wary and even suspicious. The more senior you are, the greater the number of subordinate staff who will worry over the changes you may make.

A fixed 'good-guy/gal' demeanour won't help. The fact is that you won't be able to reassure and delight all the incumbents from day one. So don't be concerned about justifying your presence. Your first loyalty is to your work. Your colleagues' behaviour will ease up as soon as your management style is established. All in good time will they discover what a gem you are. But that doesn't mean you shouldn't make all the right opening moves.

Having eased yourself in, you can start upgrading levels of business etiquette. But tread warily: old patterns of behaviour may be deeply entrenched and backed by no coherent reasons other than an embedded corporate class system or the whims of insecure predecessors.

Staff introductions

When a new executive joins a company, the first formalities to be observed are the introductions. Here, the general rule is that junior is introduced to senior. So, when introducing a manager to a director, the basic structure is: 'Mr Newman, I'd like to introduce Mr Thrust, our marketing manager.' Precedents for the use of first names are encouraged with 'Mr Alan Newman, may I introduce Mr Roland Thrust, our marketing director.' It doesn't matter in which order the names are spoken, so long as the subordinate is clearly being introduced to his superior. Women executives takes precedence over men: 'Mrs Best, may I introduce our new sales director, Mr Newman.'

When introducing yourself, as at the interview, the title 'Mr', 'Mrs' or 'Miss' should not be used. The form is, 'How do you do. My name is Somebody Somebody, office manager.' Your company position indicates whether the first name, or the second name with title, should be used in reply.

The staff themselves should welcome the newcomer pleasantly and warmly. A sincere effort to make someone new feel more at home will be remembered, and will certainly help the future relationship.

Introductions to clients

In the business hierarchy, the client is king. Even if you are the boss, you are introduced to him. 'Mr Purchase, I'd like you to meet Mr Alan Newman, our new sales director.'

> When bosses, male and female colleagues, and others are milling around it can be a demanding task for the person responsible for introducing them. But order can be maintained simply by remembering the pecking order: a junior is introduced to a senior . . . a man to a woman . . . a colleague to a client.

Addressing the boss

Unless otherwise indicated, you should always start out by calling your seniors (and their secretaries) 'Mr', 'Mrs', 'Miss' or 'Ms'. It is up to them to tell you when you should call them by their first name.

In a large company if you know the top man personally don't flaunt it. Where everyone else at your level calls him 'Mr', then in public so should you. Very often such a relationship may be resented by your peers. If neither of you mixes your work and social lives, explain accordingly. You might add – if it is true – that, if anything, he will probably be harder on you than on everyone else. If they don't believe you, there's nothing much you can do about it. Never offer or agree to use your personal relationship to have a quiet word to the boss on someone's behalf;

> A boss should take care to behave in an even-handed way in all his staff relationships. A hint of favouritism in the way certain people are addressed or treated can easily generate resentment and ill-feeling.

that will make matters worse. Steer clear of using his nickname to others, particularly if it is derogatory. From a new boy, it signifies disrespect and a wish to be a member of the herd.

Self-addressing

Precedent often dictates how someone in your position is addressed. Where and how first names are used is a matter of company tradition. If you think the company conducts such matters in a particularly starchy manner and you want to relax things, take care to consult older staff first. Some may feel they will lose credibility and respect if staff are allowed to call them by their first names. Whatever your view, pay them the respect of discussing it before making your recommendation. Having decided on a procedure, stick to it. Even when you're having a bad day, don't suddenly tell someone to call you 'Mr'; that kind of humiliation breeds deep-seated resentment.

It may be all right to call people just by their surnames at school, but after that time most people don't like it. Dropping the 'Mr' or other title can sound disrespectful and arrogant.

If the office junior happens to be third in line to the throne, there is no need to call him 'sir'. At work it is one's business seniority that counts, not one's social rank.

Tom, Dick, Harry and Luv

Many people dislike having their names abbreviated. When first introduced and unless advised otherwise, play it safely and courteously by not cutting Thomas to Tom, Richard to Dick, Gillian to Gill and so on.

Check your use of idioms: expressions like luv, pet, my dear, sweetheart and darling are ill-advised, especially from a newcomer. In many establishments they are considered passé, patronising and chauvinist, and will certainly alienate some of your female colleagues. So as not to appear to over-react, women can respond to these expressions with a simple and pleasant statement of their title and surname, or their Christian name.

Standing for your secretary

The first day may be one of the few occasions when a man stands as his secretary first enters his office. Once she has been introduced, there is of course no need to repeat the gesture regularly.

It is courteous always to greet one's secretary with a full welcome in the morning, and a pleasant acknowledgement at other times. Exchanging such social niceties as 'How are you today?' does no harm at all. Secretaries seldom complain that their boss is too polite to them.

Making the first move

Others in the company will know what your name and job are, so as soon as possible move up to par. Get a list of names, functions and extensions and take the time to phone and then call on those you have not already met – if possible in *their* offices. By taking the initiative, you are paying them a compliment and signalling your acknowledgment of their important positions in the organisation.

Listening

In all affairs, be they business, courtship or war, the first essential is information. Check with the training or personnel department about telephone procedures, coffee breaks, security and so on. Ask them or the office manager about such conventions as wearing jacket and tie when moving about the building, whether men stand when a woman/ senior manager enters an office and so on. Your adherence or otherwise to these rules will have an influence on others' attitude and conduct, so always keep your eyes open and observe what other people do.

> Before brandishing a new broom, learn how the old one worked by reviewing the company's customs, protocol and rules of etiquette.

Gossiping

Tuning in to the gossip network is one way of learning about a new company. But it is usually subjective and rarely reliable. Whenever you hear something that may affect the company, it is wise neither to believe it nor to repeat it until you have seen evidence for yourself. Certainly, an executive should resist joining in. It is demeaning to oneself and destructive to one's standing to make derogatory or facetious remarks about staff and colleagues. (See also Chapter 8.)

21

Addressing memos

It is unrealistic to expect everyone from office boy to directors to know who you are from day one. So for the first couple of weeks, head your memos and electronic mail with your full name, title and job. Wherever possible, your first internal memo to each colleague should mention how pleased you were to meet him, as well as some other friendly and encouraging comment.

Restrain yourself from launching a paper chase. A memo-man runs the risk of isolating himself. Ask yourself, particularly when you are still settling in, whether or not a personal meeting would be more effective. If the subject needs to go on record, a meeting can be followed by a short report.

Saying thank you

One of the first traditions to establish (if it isn't there already) is that of thanking employees for their good work. It is not enough that they are paid. They need personal appreciation for their function in life – everyone does. And you will get greater dedication from them in the future (see Chapter 3). That does not, however, absolve you of the responsibility of distributing tangible largesse at Christmas or on your secretary's birthday.

> 'Courtesy is the lubrication of life. In the world of business, knowing how to ensure success on a personal level is the most important area of business knowledge.'
>
> RONNIE JACOBSON, General Manager of Public Affairs and Marketing at the London Chamber of Commerce.

Chapter 3

STAFF COMMUNICATIONS

ONCE upon a time, God became heartily sick of people continually whingeing about their lives. So he commanded them all to place their problems in sacks, throw them into a circle and each take out someone else's. With what relish did they pack their sacks and hurl them onto the pile! But after a short while examining the options, they all took thier own sacks back.

That Yiddish morality tale is a valuable one for those pressurised executives who take it for granted that their problems are more profound than everyone else's and who don't adequately take into account the pressures under which their staff work. They don't appear to care much about them either.

Better managers are more observant; they recognise the trials and ordeals of more junior staff. They know that stress can be reduced and morale strengthened by remembering and acknowledging that no one's problems are, to him, less serious than anyone else's. And that, whatever the weight of his burden, he is sensitive to criticism and responsive to encouragement.

Making people feel better

Workplace rituals can cover smoking, ventilation, office or plant tidiness, display material, heating levels and so on. If you are a new manager with the power to take decisions about these practices, you should ascertain everyone's views on them and then, if necessary, adjust and update them for the welfare of the majority.

If you feel the presence of petty rivalries, personal aversions and other such issues, try to discover the reasons. They could be based on fundamental working problems that you may be able to resolve. They won't go away by themselves, and unless tactfully confronted they will continue to affect morale.

It can be valuable to hold occasional meetings with staff to keep them informed and to elicit their views on issues that concern them.

A practical therapy in a chronically bad working atmosphere is to make a habit of pleasantly greeting everyone you see for the first time in the day. It's a small gesture, but it could catch on, and who knows where it could lead? . . . people might even start smiling at one another!

> 'In today's electronic age, it is easy to overlook the simple courtesies between people in business. It would be a tragedy if the world became more efficient at the cost of human relationships.'
>
> JOE CORR, Sales and Marketing Director (N. Europe) for WordStar International.

Personal notes

Working with a large number of people makes it difficult to remember the particular circumstances that govern each of their lives. So you may find it useful to make notes in your diary reminding you when to ask about any domestic problems your staff may have mentioned to you. Enquiring discretely and briefly about a relation's illness, a home move, a child's school progress and other such concerns, demonstrates your care and consideration for the people around you.

Personal questions

Executives are often approached by staff on matters of a personal nature. The best policy is to try not to get involved. Taking too close an interest in the personal life of a member of staff may undermine the confidence of others. You could be accused of favouritism and they of toadying. If possible, divert the problem to the personnel manager.

Favours

When extra cooperation or help is needed from above, full-frontal flattery may not be the best approach: and anyway it's usually a transparent and short-term strategy. Let's say you want to get through to the chairman via his iron-clad secretary. A male who tries floating the 'How's the world's most beautiful secretary?' sting, would probably be considered an ineffectual sexist. Far better the approach with built-in esteem like 'If anyone can help me get through to the chairman, I know you can . . .'.

Or the respectful 'Did the chairman by any chance mention to you when he would be available to take a call?' One could add the charmingly insidious: 'Thank you, I'm grateful for all the trouble you are taking.' And remember to thank her again, afterwards, for fixing the appointment.

Thank you, too

Do you know which characteristic Genghis Khan had in common with Al Capone? Neither paid much attention to their 'p's and q's'. They probably felt that their vocation didn't call for such everyday courtesies. There are those we all know today who apply a similarly cretinous approach and amass equally few admirers. Grunts may have been good enough for heads of hordes, they aren't for business managers.

> In business, expressing appreciation is vital. To state the obvious: it is a way of acknowledging that without the people around you, you wouldn't be able to succeed in your job.

Everyone deserves to be thanked for his contribution to the daily slog, regardless of his rank and function. Should such courtesies be a low priority among certain reprobates of your management staff, you should make a point in their presence of thanking people sincerely for everything they do for you. The others will soon catch on.

'Allocating responsibility'

Being secure means never having to give orders. No one should have to bellow commands to get them followed. Whether you are addressing the office junior or a senior aide, you get a better response when, instead of giving orders, you *allocate responsibility*. It makes people feel important. For example, 'Guy, draw me up a full list of our software suppliers and make sure no one's left off' is less effective than 'Guy, would you take responsibility for drafting a complete list of our software suppliers, please.'

Democracy at work

The executive who grovels under the boss's heel and then treads all over his underlings is displaying his inadequacies. The successful executive does not operate a sliding scale of attitudes toward employees, peers and bosses. Nor does he treat males more chummily than their female peers, because that isn't a positive trait either.

Secretary care

Rapport is the most important aspect when choosing one's own secretary. If that is absent, the working relationship will eventually break down.

Having engaged her, a good secretary should be considered as part of a team. She will have a worth far in excess of her administrative talents. Taking time during the day – first thing, if possible – to discuss appointments and other business activities is a good way of maintaining smooth communications and aiding efficiency.

Respect works both ways. As a secretary supports a boss's decisions, so you should support those she must make in your absence. You should not publicly blame or criticise her if she made the wrong one. Instead, point out, behind closed doors, a better way of handling such a situation in future.

A secretary's loyalty is shown not only in her job performance, but also in maintaining confidentiality and restraining from gossip. If she is unhappy with some aspect of their working relationship, she must discuss the grievance with her boss as soon as possible, rather than becoming moody and resentful.

Finally, there are few better ways that a boss can improve his secretary's morale, commitment and loyalty than by expressing his appreciation for the job she is doing.

'The competitive edge in the 1990s is achieved by gaining the commitment of all levels of staff. To achieve this commitment requires the creation of people-centred organisations. The central role of people in organisations will be reinforced if high standards of dealing with each other are acquired on a day-to-day basis, over the telephone and in face to face contact. What is equally important is that the customer will notice the difference, so helping the bottom line.'

ALISTAIR GRAHAM, Director of the Industrial Society.

Customer consideration

Clients are worthy of special consideration, but that doesn't mean behaving obsequiously and laughing thunderously at rotten jokes. Such behaviour is perfidious, difficult to keep up and creates tension.

On the other hand, one should also be careful of over-familiarity with clients, knowing that one day it might not be appropriate and may even be resented.

Clients should decide on the means of address and make the first move towards informality. Otherwise, they should be addressed as 'Mr', 'Mrs' or 'Ms', until you know them well. Having established first name relationships, don't take it for granted that it is acceptable for the privilege to be taken up by more junior staff.

Volume orders

When someone shouts at an employee, it humiliates, demeans and antagonises – it embarrasses everyone and impresses no one. Shouting is tantamount to swearing at a high pitch. Most people dislike it and few respect the shouter. It is ultimately ineffectual. It is also exremely disrespectful and terrible manners.

If a manager shouts more than a couple of times a week, it may look to others that he is losing his grip.

Memo lore

The following is the memo-equivalent of shouting: 'The front office is a pigsty. I hold all of you responsible for ensuring that it is clean and tidy before the chairman's visit this afternoon.' The response to this kind of missive will probably be resentful, and the resulting atmosphere sullen.

The executive using the following approach gets a sparkling response: 'I can see from the chaotic state of the front office that you are all working flat out. I appreciate it. The chairman is visiting this afternoon, so would you please do the best you can to ensure that the area is perfectly clean and tidy for 2pm, when he is due to arrive. With thanks . . .'

An office is not a happy one in which the boss is a memo-man who continually uses memos to carp about others' below-par performance, or to complain about his own workload or working conditions. The staff are even less inspired by a memo with a condescending tone.

Memos are not the best medium for criticism. Far better to tender criticism in person, to give the alleged offender a chance to defend himself (see also Chapter 7).

Memos are an effective medium for encouraging employees and for recognising and praising success – with copies widely circulated. They are an effective and courteous way of keeping staff updated on such issues as company activities, and for putting on record the reasons for changes in plans or for delays in implementing them. The sender should take care to include every appropriate employee on his circulation list.

In an office with delicate egos to consider, memos should be carefully drafted so as not to make others feel threatened or resentful. It's thoughtful occasionally to end a memo with a note of your pleasure at the results being achieved by the whole department or company team.

Performance and productivity

Where there is a need to upgrade performance and productivity, you should start by involving all relevant members of staff. They must consider themselves allies in the enterprise; failing to take them into your confidence may cause resentment and resistance. Departmental incentive schemes should be handled with tact, particularly if there is a chance that staff may sense the inference that they are not doing enough.

Acknowledging hard work and success

It is very important for a company to show evidence of the trouble it takes over a staff celebration such as the annual office outing or party. It should not be a routine, predictable event, but a sincere and original gesture of gratitude for good work and loyalty throughout the year.

If possible, a short speech should be made by the senior executive, with a reference to the teamwork that contributed to the company's achievements. An even shorter speech can be made in return by a senior member of the staff, in which thanks for the evening are expressed.

'The most important business investment of all is in people and in developing their abilities to communicate with customers and to work well with one another. Without that, all the other investments will be a complete waste.'

RICHARD BRANSON, Chairman of the Virgin Group of Companies.

Chapter 4

TELEPHONE CULTURE

COMPANIES spend huge amounts polishing and projecting their images: in the media, at conferences, sales presentations and in warm and friendly-looking brochures. Then someone blows every penny by answering the telephone in an off-hand, uninterested and impersonal manner.

The phone is a selling instrument. It is used to sell not only goods, services and ideas, but also prestige.

Even if 99 per cent of telephone calls we receive are from people who are selling rather than buying, we ourselves always have one important thing to sell – our reputation. The way calls are handled supports or mars the reputation of the entire organisation – shareholders, board of directors, employees, agents and all.

The telephone is our primary connection to a world crammed full of business opportunities, so it is in a company's interests to ensure that everyone with access to one uses it with aptitude and as much grace as they can muster.

Of equal importance in terms of morale and performance is the quality of telephone relationships between a company's employees.

The right of reply

Just giving the name of the company without a greeting doesn't enhance the company image one bit.

For most switchboard operators, variations on a theme of 'X and Co., may I help you?' are about right. Some say 'X and Co. . . . how may I help you?' Others even 'Thank you for calling X and Co. Gary speaking. How can I help you?' The most important thing is to use a bright and positive tone that demonstrates that the call is welcome.

Hello

'Hello' is the call sign of the indifferent, irritated, irritating, bored and untrained individual. When delivered in a flat, peremptory tone it makes the caller feel unwelcome and unimpressed, if not defensive and petulant. 'Hello' is never enough when one answers the phone. It doesn't identify, it doesn't inform, it doesn't sell.

To unenlightened users 'Hello' is the substance of all telephone greetings. Together with 'Goodbye' it is the beginning and end of their telephone technique. It can also be the beginning and end of a company's positive contact with new clients.

Who's there?

Most mono-syllabicists probably haven't the faintest notion of the effect their telephone manner has on people. They probably make outgoing calls in the same wooden style, for instance, 'Mr Prospect there?' Instead of the smart: 'Good morning, it's Gerry Mander of Certain Sales here. May I speak to Mr Prospect, please?'

Fobbing and bouncing

If a caller wants to be put through to someone who is engaged, he shouldn't be kept holding on without being told what is happening. Whoever takes the call should try to return to him frequently, and in any case he should never be left fuming in limbo for longer than half a minute. Apologies should be made for keeping him waiting and he should be offered the option of continuing to hold or of having someone ring him back. (Only as a last resort should he be advised to call back.) One should try not to use such glib phrases as 'I'll do that *for you*' . . . 'I'll ask him to return your call, *for you*;' the emphasis is wrong, as the caller may consider that calling him back is primarily to the other firm's advantage.

The call's yours

If an unmanned phone rings, it should be handled on the lines of: 'Don Leaver's phone, Henry Stay speaking, can I help you?' That demonstrates care and professionalism. One should then take personal responsibility for the caller getting through to his destination or until all options have been tried. We have all experienced the 'Hold on a minute' prelude to a dead line or a run-around, and we don't think a lot of the company that allows it to happen.

'The first and often the most lasting impression that anyone has of your company is through the phone. It is much more than a communications device. It is an opportunity to create a customer relationship which is beyond the reach of your competition.'

MARTIN SHIELDS, Managing Director of Merit Direct, one of the UK's leading telemarketing and database marketing companies.

Phone tone

Tone and attitude are all important. Your secretary's attitude may be honeyed and melodious when speaking to you, but how is she to everyone else? Have you discussed telephone procedures with her? If not, listen in: she may be harming your reputation with a brusque manner.

Some employees may simply not appreciate that it is just as important to be courteous to people on the phone as it is when face to face. It's worth investing time with all your staff checking their phone manner. The importance of courteous telephone techniques should be explained fully to those below par.

Once they understand that, you can suggest the following 'Phone Projection' techniques, which will help improve the most repellent or anaesthetising of telephone tones.

Phone projection

Posture is important. Slumping over the phone devitalises the voice. Sitting straight can add dynamism to it. And if you want to sound more assertive, stand up.

Smile – albeit faintly. It may seem a quaint idea, but it works. When you smile, your voice sounds more pleasing.

Check your mood – the telephone magnifies any emotion in your voice. People instantaneously sense tedium, rancour etc. and they resent it; whereas in nearly all cases they will respond positively to a pleasantly animated voice.

Check your tone – the fact that you are under crushing pressure is of no material interest to most callers. Their call is more important to them than is the prospect of an imminent cataclysm to you.

Don't speak on the phone with food or a cigarette in your mouth. It can sound unpleasant and disrespectful.

Give the caller your name; ask for his and use it. It establishes a relationship and a future contact.

When providing information, don't speak too quickly. Repeat numbers, and ask the caller to confirm that he is satisfied with your answers and has understood them.

Allow people to finish what they have to say. Don't interrupt them in mid-sentence, particularly when there is a dispute. Quick-fire rebuttals stoke up animosity.

Short and sweet

The telephone key word is courtesy. Then come clarity and brevity, which should not be mistaken for volume and abruptness. We never know how busy or otherwise the people we call are. So 'How are you and the family' is a fine preamble, although an analysis of why someone kept hooking his tee-shot last weekend may not be a priority topic at that moment.

To sound good on the phone:

- Do sit up straight throughout the conversation
- Do smile while you are talking
- Don't sound bored or irritable
- Don't sound pressurised
- Don't eat or smoke while on the phone
- Stand up to be more assertive
- Do exchange names and use them in conversation
- Don't rattle off information too fast
- Don't interrupt the other person
- Remember: courtesy, clarity, brevity

Look who's calling

If you want your secretary to put people off, she should never say 'He's too busy' or just 'He's out.' She should give a reason why you cannot get to the phone, apologise, and ask if you can call him back when you are able.

Defusing rudeness

Some callers are intimidating. When they bellow 'Is he in?' to the average secretary, followed by a stream of indecorous expressions, it will probably unnerve her. If she is young and inexperienced, she may

believe that anyone as forthright (that is, rude) as that must be important and will not want to further upset him by asking too many
questions.

It is her boss's responsibility to make the staff aware that if a caller –
regardless of his status – is rude without any provocation, they have his
permission to terminate the call and should then report the conversation
to him.

If a secretary wishes to deal with an irate caller, she should first slow
the tempo, starting with 'I'll just see if he is in. May I ask who is calling?
. . . Mr Himmler. Of what company/department, please? . . . Thank
you. And will he know what you are calling about?'

No one, however rude, should be abandoned for long periods. If a
secretary cannot locate her boss, the caller should not be kept hanging in
limbo during the search. She must continually report her progress and
offer the caller the option of being called back or leaving a message. In
all circumstances, she must apologise for keeping him waiting.

Misuse

In properly run companies, the telephone should not be used for repri-
manding people or sacking them. Nor was it designed to communicate
heart-felt congratulations or significant promotions.

Warning calls

When you call someone for an important discussion, at what turns out
to be an inconvenient time for him, ask when he will have the necessary
time free for an uninterrupted dialogue. Describe the kind of information you may need, so he can have it to hand when you call back.

If you wish to make a particularly important call, wherever possible
give the other party advance warning so he can set aside the time, and
will be able to give you his full attention. You owe it to yourself and the
person you are calling to make proper preparations. If specific information is likely to be needed, have it to hand so you don't have to shout out
for your secretary, or trek across the office and plough through filing
cabinets while he's hanging on.

If someone comes on the line with a potentially lengthy call for which
you may not have time, inform him as early as possible how long you can
talk and give him the option to call back at an agreed hour.

When your call isn't really necessary, but ho hum, you've got a bit of
time on your hands, don't make it. It could interrupt someone's flow.
For the same reason, if you have a number of facts to impart, don't

phone them through one at a time as they reach you. Wait until you have them all together and then make one call.

Calling personally

Unless you are juggling with meetings or lists of calls, it is more effectual to dial your own calls rather than have your secretary do it. On a modern console it usually involves only a single tap.

> Dialling direct rather than through your secretary has a subtle psychological effect on the person being called. It is a compliment to the recipient, signifying the caller's respect and particular interest.

On the mark

When a call is dialled on your behalf, it is courteous to be ready to speak immediately. If not, just think of the basket of negatives awaiting you. The recipient feels he is being kept hanging on unnecessarily while you finish messing around with something you should have got shot of before calling. He will presume you do not regard him as particularly important. As time passes, irritation will blossom into thriving resentment. Is it any wonder that keeping people hanging on may earn you a 'Yes?' – which is even further down the sliding scale than 'Hello'.

Mobile phone lines

What is the difference between a Wild West saloon of the 1890s and the Ritz Hotel Restaurant of the 1990s? In the saloon you had to park your shooting irons before you were allowed in, and before they let you into the Ritz you have to park your mobile telephone.

Considered a huge convenience by owners but a deadly nuisance by many others within earshot, the mobile telephone needs to be used with care and consideration. Not for nothing was it dubbed the 'poser-phone', dating from when it was a very flash item, taken into meetings in the hope that it would ring and impress people. Nowadays the novelty has worn off, and a receiving and dialling code of behaviour is required so as not to annoy others.

As drumming fingers and shuddering sighs may illustrate, taking or making such phone calls during meetings, conferences and business gatherings is not appreciated. So the phone should be switched off or, if so equipped, the 'call diversion' facility switched on.

If a crucial call is expected which has nothing to do with the meeting, permission to take it should be sought in advance from the principal people present.

Making and receiving calls on a mobile phone during someone else's meeting can indicate the user's diverse priorities, so it may not make a positive impression on the assembly. In nearly all circumstances the user should withdraw from the room, or at least from the immediate vicinity, so as not to interrupt proceedings.

'Enormous strides are being taken in telecommunications to bring greater speed and efficiency to people's business and private lives. We must never lose sight, however, of the importance of human relationships in communications.'

PETER VAN CUYLENBURG, Chief Executive of Mercury Communications.

Personal calls

Unless by special arrangement, making private calls on company phones is actually regarded by some people as stealing – or, more elegantly stated, embezzlement. Consequently, just about everyone with access to a company telephone could sooner or later be an embezzler. And with electronic devices now able to record phone numbers dialled, and with the introduction of itemised bills, unauthorised calls can easily be traced. So rather than risk embarrassment, employees should ascertain their company's 'personal call' policy and act accordingly.

It is vital for employers to make it perfectly clear what those rules are. Among other things, they should include (a) the maximum number and type (e.g. local only) of calls – if any – allowed; (b) how far company-related and 'sorry-dear-I'm-having-to-work-late' calls can be stretched; and (c) what arrangements are available for reimbursing the company.

Receiving lengthy personal calls also presents problems, particularly where an employer, quite understandably, considers that people are being paid for every minute of their time.

It is understandable, too, that bosses (not to mention visiting customers) are unnerved when they see the company phone being used for courting, personal arguments and gossip.

. . . All good reasons why personal calls should be kept short and sweet.

Chapter 5

CORRESPONDENCE

M UCH of today's business correspondence brims with tortuous formality. Many writers do not seem to be in touch with the principle that letters are a way of communicating between human beings and should be written as such.

In 'the professions', certain sectors of the civil service and in too many areas of commercial life, such relics as 'ult', 'inst', 'your esteemed communication' and the ironic 'We remain your obedient servant' can still be found, and obscure more than they advise. Even where such Dickensian phrases have died out, they have been replaced by equally tedious modern jargon and cliché. Such language not only patronises but also metaphorically distances the writer from the recipient.

There is actually no real difficulty in writing good business letters. The key is the same as for all business communications – courtesy, clarity and brevity.

The style of a business letter is not only an indication of the writer's personal regard for the recipient, but is a testimonial to a company's culture and professionalism.

Notes on letters

Business letters should be typed or printed. Personal letters should be handwritten.

Business letters, however short, should be laid out centrally on standard company letterhead.

Take care with alterations, including those made with correction fluid; they could indicate the level of importance the sender and his secretary attach to the letter or to the recipient. The appearance of a letter is the responsibility of the writer. However efficient the secretary may be, the writer must take the time to read his letters and check for small mistakes before signing them.

> In checking for errors in one's correspondence, a reputation for sloppiness may be the least of the repercussions – ask any libel lawyer.

Names and titles are often important to their bearers and should be checked and confirmed. Spelling names incorrectly or getting titles wrong indicates that the writer is inefficient or insensitive or both.

> *Letter writer's checklist:*
> - Type business letters on letterhead
> - Hand-write personal letters
> - Visible alterations say you don't care
> - It's your responsibility to check for mistakes
> - Get names and titles right and correctly spelt

Compliment slips

Items sent between businesses (other than for general goods deliveries, of course) should be accompanied by some communication on paper, usually a compliment slip. But these slips should be used only for perfunctory messages. If more than one sentence is required, it belongs in a letter rather than bunched on to a compliment slip.

When a compliment slip is sent to known business associates a short message should be written or typed on it.

Other than to close colleagues, it is inadvisable, not to say risky, to hand-write strategic information on a compliment slip, as the sender often has no record of its content or proof of despatch.

Thank you notes

A letter expressing appreciation after you have enjoyed another company's hospitality should be on company letterhead. But a prim 'Mr and Mrs C. Legs thank you for your kind hospitality on the occasion of your company centenary' has as much warmth as a parking fine. Furthermore, it obviously came via Mr Legs' secretary.

It would be more courteous if Mr Legs were to send a handwritten note with a personal touch, such as 'Thank you very much for inviting us to your centenary celebration the other night. Joan and I enjoyed it very much. We look forward to seeing you soon.'

Not on company paper

Personal letters are not the only things that shouldn't be written on company headed paper. Among the others are:

- Political or charitable fund-raising

- Investment activities unconnected with the company

- Legal matters unconnected with the company

- Letters asking for non-company services and favours, for example requesting private membership of a golf club

- Letters of complaint unconnected with the company, such as to your local council, the gas board or the editor of a newspaper.

- Letters of congratulation or condolence for personal achievement or loss – even to company employees.

Dear . . . Yours

There are any number of combinations of opening and closing salutations. A frequent mistake is following 'Dear Sir' with 'Yours sincerely,' and 'Dear Mr Smith' with 'Yours faithfully'. The rule, however, is simple: 'Yours sincerely' is used when writing to a named person, while 'Yours faithfully' is used with 'Dear Sir' or 'Dear Madam'.

These are some of the many acceptable combinations (see also pages 43–6):

For someone you know well, say a business colleague with whom you have a close working relationship:

Start: Dear Jonathan,
End: Yours sincerely, *or* Sincerely,

For a person you have met once, perhaps a customer or executive with whom you are establishing a close working relationship:

Start: Dear Jonathan Hope,
End: Yours sincerely, *or* Yours very truly,

For a new acquaintance with whom contact has been only by letter:

Start: Dear Mr Hope,
End: Yours sincerely,

To functionaries with whom no relationship has been established, including civic officials, bank managers etc.

Start: Dear Sir, *or* Dear Madam,
End: Yours faithfully, *or* Yours truly,

As a last resort:

Start: Dear Sir or Madam,
End: Yours faithfully,

> 'There are three rules in business writing: Be clear, be concise, be human. Anyone who does not keep to these rules is living in the 1970s.'
>
> CHRISSIE MAHER, Director of the Plain English Campaign.

Starting a letter

A formal business letter to a colleague with whom you are on first-name terms is enhanced when it begins with a personal comment, such as an enquiry about his health, his family or a current activity. For instance:

Dear James,

I hope you have recovered from your cold/your daughter did well in her exams. I just wanted to confirm the details discussed at our meeting last Tuesday.

. . . And ending

In normal circumstances, there is every reason to end a business letter on a pleasant note. Rather than 'We anticipate a prompt reply', why not 'I look forward to receiving your comments as soon as you are able'?
Then mix and match:

'With best wishes' or 'With kindest regards' – with or without 'Yours sincerely'. 'Yours etc.' means nothing.

The name of the signatory should be typed under the signature.

To 'p.p.' or not to 'p.p.'

Having your secretary sign 'p.p.' (*per procurationem:* for and on behalf of) for you is perfectly acceptable when a brief note of explanation is added, such as: '(Signed in Mr Angel's absence)' or '(Dictated by phone from Mr Angel, on overseas assignment from 23 to 29 June).'

Words of caution

- It is not prudent to be rude by letter. Tempers cool, circumstances change, misunderstandings are settled. But words on paper remain. They will probably be regretted, perhaps not today or tomorrow, but one day.

- Never write anything in a letter that has the faintest chance of being libellous. A derogatory comment made in a fit of temper can cost the signatory dear in friction and damages.

- Resist making jibes in letters about mutal associates. Remember that the wittier the comment, the more likely it will be repeated by your correspondent or someone in his office. A libellous quip has astonishing velocity and endurance and can carry you and your company straight into court and disrepute.

Save paper, lose business

It may seem expeditious at the time, but it is bad manners to return someone's original letter with your reply scrawled on the bottom. For one thing, people may think you don't regard their letter or themselves as significant. That may indeed be your view today. But discourtesy ultimately reaps its own harvest.

Dealing with unsolicited mail

If you really are interested in a time-share villa in Novosibirsk, or lust after a porridge dispensing machine, or can't wait to own a Swiss knife that can extract acorns from cuckoo clocks, that's fine. On the other hand, you may prefer to take a stand against junk mail.

Unfortunately, short of illegal computer hacking it is unlikely you will be able to remove your name from all the lists which are sold to direct mail firms. There is, however, a polite way that will help: devise three or four standard replies for the more persistent and irrelevant types of missives. For example:

To charities:
'Thank you for sending me news of your latest appeal. This company supports a number of charities regularly and we are not considering expanding that number at present. I would be grateful if you would remove our name from your list until further notice.' (Of course, if this is not the case, you may wish your company to select a number of charities to support before sending the letter.)

To property companies:
'Thank you for your letter regarding your selection of low-priced business premises in Greenfields new town business park. We have no plans to change or add to our business premises in the foreseeable future. Would you therefore please remove our name from your mailing list until further notice.'

To job applicants:
'Thank you very much for writing about a position with this company. Unfortunately there are no vacancies at present for someone of your qualifications. We will be keeping your letter on file and should a position arise that we think would suit you, we will certainly contact you. We appreciate your contacting us and thank you again for your interest in our company.'

Complaints (see also Chapter 11)

Grievances against the company should be dealt with by letter from the highest possible level. Even though they may be patently unjustified or plainly vindictive, they must be handled with care and in detail. Failure to manage them promptly and adequately may provoke letters to even higher authorities and will incur even more time-consuming correspondence.

Never answer a rude letter of complaint with an insult. Maintain the dignity and status of your company at all costs; offer to investigate the complaint and, having done so, reply politely and in full.

Letters to the media

Unjustified complaints or criticisms in the media should be responded to by the managing director or the senior responsible executive in consultation with a lawyer and, if possible, a competent PR executive. It is useful to phone the editor to discuss your rebuttal before it is drafted, and your lawyer before it is sent.

The folding business
Thousands of pounds' worth of design work, printing technology and communications expertise have gone into your pristine, perfectly drafted, perfectly printed letter. Then someone folds it sloppily and it's all wasted. Neatly and crisply folded letters have the vital finishing touch and take only a second longer to achieve than the disorderly variety.

Fax

Facsimile has invaded many of the former preserves of letter, telex, telegraph and telephone. Despite the often urgent nature of their content, they should include all the courtesies reserved for other forms of written communication. Whether or not they are printed on standard company forms, the language used in a business-to-business fax should be that of a letter.

Faxes should not be used to respond to letters which do not require an urgent reply, or to formal invitations.

Boilerplate text indicating that the recipient must phone a specific number if the transmission is incomplete should be drafted as a request, not a command.

Faxes are increasingly used for unsolicited marketing purposes. The law to date has been unclear as to the rights of the sender to 'steal' other people's stationery for their own promotion. If you do not wish to be sold to in this way, you should write or fax the company concerned asking them to remove your name from their list. If they fail to do so, they may be breaking the law.

Upwardly mobile letters

Letters to senior establishment figures should be addressed as follows. They all, except for the Pope, should be signed off 'Yours sincerely'. (Names or places have been added to titles to clarify usage.)

Royalty

Letters to HM The Queen/HRH The Duke of Edinburgh/HM The Queen Mother (when the sender is not previously known to them), are all addressed to the relevant Private Secretary:
The Private Secretary to Her Majesty The Queen/His Royal Highness The Duke of Edinburgh/Her Majesty The Queen Mother
All begin: Dear Private Secretary

Letters to HRH The Prince of Wales/HRH The Princess of Wales/
HRH The Princess Royal/HRH Princess Margaret are addressed to:
His Royal Highness The Prince of Wales/Her Royal Highness The
Princess of Wales/Her Royal Highness The Princess Royal/Her Royal
Highness Princess Margaret, Countess of Snowdon
All begin: Your Royal Highness

Letters to royal dukes/duchesses are addressed to:
His/Her Royal Highness, The Duke/Duchess of York
All begin: Your Royal Highness

Peers, baronets, knights
Letters to dukes/duchesses are addressed to:
The Duke/Duchess of Oxland
They begin with: Dear Duke/Duchess of Oxland, or Dear Duke/
Duchess

Letters to marquesses/marchionesses, earls/countesses, viscounts/
viscountesses are addressed to:
The Marquess/Marchioness of Parsham, The Earl/Countess of Satham,
The Viscount/Viscountess Tatham
All begin: Dear Lord/Lady Parsham/Satham/Tatham

Letters to barons/baronesses are addressed to:
The Lord Makepiece/The Lady Makepiece
They begin: Dear Lord/Lady Makepiece

Letters to baronets and their wives are addressed to:
Sir Anthony Dewit, Bt/Lady Dewit
They begin: Dear Sir Anthony/Lady Dewit

Letters to life peers are addressed to:
The Lord Fireback/The Lady Fireback
They begin: Dear Lord/Lady Fireback

Letters to knights and their wives are addressed to:
Sir Charles Counter/Lady Counter
They begin: Dear Sir Charles/Lady Counter

Letters to hereditary peeresses (direct line) are addressed to:
The Countess of Downe
They begin: Dear Lady Downe

Letters to life peeresses are addressed to:
Baroness Chambers
They begin: Dear Lady Chambers

Letters to dames are addressed to:
Dame Flora Lynch
They begin: Dear Dame Flora

The clergy

Letters to (Anglican) lord archbishops are addressed to:
The Most Revd and Rt Hon. the Lord Archbishop of Canterbury/York
They begin: Dear Archbishop

Letters to (Anglican) bishops are addressed to:
The Right Revd the Lord Bishop of Birmington, (The Bishop of
London is addressed as: The Rt Revd and Rt Hon. the Lord Bishop of
London)
They all begin: Dear Bishop

Letters to Anglican vicars are addressed to:
Reverend M. Waters
They begin: Reverend Sir

Letters to Roman Catholic priests are addressed to:
Father Miller
They begin: Dear Reverend Father

Letters to Church of Scotland ministers are addressed to:
Father McMillan
They begin: Dear Father McMillan

Letters to The Pope are addressed to:
His Holiness The Pope
They begin: Your Holiness *or* Most Holy Father
The letter should end: I have the honour to remain your Holiness's most
devoted and obedient child (*or* most humble child). A non-Roman
Catholic may replace 'child' by 'servant'.

Letters to (Roman Catholic) archbishops are addressed to:
His Grace the Archbishop of Beltown
They begin: Dear Archbishop *or* Your Grace

Letters to The Chief Rabbi are addressed to:
The Chief Rabbi Mr Emanuel Foreman
They begin: Dear Chief Rabbi

Politicians (personal and official letters)
Letters to the Prime Minister are addressed to:
The Rt Hon. Paddy Sutch MP
They begin: Dear Prime Minister

Letters to the Chancellor of the Exchequer are addressed to:
The Rt Hon. James Sargeant, PC, MP
They begin: Dear Chancellor

Letters to Secretaries of State are addressed to:
The Rt Hon. Glynis Morris, PC, MP
The Home Secretary/Foreign Secretary etc.
They begin: Dear Secretary of State/Home Secretary/Foreign Secretary
etc.

Letters to ministers are addressed to:
Title *or* Peter Dough, Esq., MP
They begin: Dear Minister

Letters to backbenchers are addressed to:
Thomas Flack Esq, MP
They begin: Dear Mr Flack

Local government
(NB Don't confuse a lady mayor with a lady mayoress – the latter is the
'consort' of her husband, the mayor, while the former is mayor in her
own right)
Letters to lord and lady mayors are addressed to:
The Rt Hon. the Lord Mayor of Belfast/Cardiff/Dublin/London/York
and for other cities:
The Right Worshipful the Lord Mayor of . . .
They begin: Dear Lord Mayor (including Lady Mayors)

Letters to lady mayoresses are addressed to:
The Lady Mayoress of . . .
They begin: Dear Lady Mayoress

Letters to mayors/mayoresses (*or* mayor's consort) of the following places only are addressed to:
The Worshipful the Mayor/Mayoress of Hastings/Hythe/Liverpool/New Romney/Rye
and letters to mayors/mayoresses (*or* mayor's consort) of other places are addressed to:
The Worshipful the Mayor/Lady Mayoress of (Borough or equivalent)
They all begin: Dear Mr Mayor/Madam Mayoress

See also Chapter 18.

Chapter 6

Personal Relationships in the Workplace

DON'T work on sexual relationships during business hours. Certainly not on extra-marital ones. That should be all there is to this chapter.

Instead this is likely to be one of the most-thumbed sections. One survey after another confirms that apart from the job itself, sexual relationships at work is the leading topic of interest and conversation, not to mention participation. From filing cabinet to tea dispenser, the office and factory floor are seen as the domain of the lustful predator.

The problems of sex in the workplace have been exacerbated recently by the increase in the number of women executives. This has engendered a relatively new source of attraction, that born of mutual esteem and regard between male and female peers.

And yet the workplace can be a calamitous location for illicit sexual pursuits. Career prospects can be placed seriously at risk on top of the potential for widespread emotional destruction. But since when did routine advice dampen sexual ardour? So it is as well to observe certain damage limitation techniques to cover both routine workplace dalliances and the more hazardous extra-marital liaisons.

The facts of working life

When people work in close physical proximity there will inevitably be those who are attracted to one another, and if the attraction evolves into action the affair must be negotiated discreetly. The first rule is that the workplace is not the location for intimate manoeuvres. It can be offensive and embarrassing to others at work for a couple to be seen seriously kissing or embracing.

The perils of workplace sex

For obvious reasons, sleeping around is now far less acceptable than ever before. People making themselves freely available for casual sex need to have their heads examined, at least.

Apart from that, overt promiscuity is professional suicide. It can destroy the respect of one's employers and peers and will ultimately frustrate all forms of upward mobility. It establishes one as conniving and lacking in loyalty and decorum, and it's even worse if you are considered successful at it.

A serious career can be badly damaged by wide-ranging and indiscreet sexual activity.

> 'Time and time again our clients of both sexes tell us they would never have an affair at work because they don't want to risk their careers. I think that sums up the dangers in a nutshell.'
>
> STELLA SLOAN, Managing Director of the Heather Jenner Marriage Bureau.

Avoiding scandal

Workplace romances of any kind have their drawbacks, particularly as a close relationship between two people can create resentment and jealousy among others. Overt liaisons can leave the participants open to a number of accusations, including favouritism, exclusivity, lack of concentration and diminished dedication to work. Their dallying is also inclined to create awkward situations for everyone, in particular their superiors.

All right, if you must

There are some basic edicts, founded on rudimentary good manners, to help those who, despite all good intentions and the advice given in this chapter, can't help themselves. Typically, they all begin with don't . . .

- Don't flaunt your affair in front of your colleagues. Intimate exchanges of any kind should be avoided in business hours.

- Don't let running the affair come before running your job. Your company pays you, so it has first call on your time and talents.

- Don't exchange sultry glances across crowded rooms – heat spreads and is noticed.

- Don't believe people who say 'Good luck to you.'

- Don't let the emotional ups and downs caused by your affair affect the way you deal with colleagues. You may not be aware of your fluctuating moods, but they will feel the direct effects of them.

- Don't laugh suggestively when talking to one another on the phone.

- Don't arrange quiet encounters during working hours. Such trysts are inclined to build in duration, frequency and conspicuousness.

- Don't both arrive at work complaining of tiredness, backache etc. Keep your symptoms to yourself – they are grist to the gossip's mill.

- Don't discuss your affair with anyone. If you are bursting for a confidant, make it a true friend sworn to secrecy, someone whose discretion you trust and who will not betray your confidences under any circumstances. They will probably look for someone with the same qualities to tell. And so on.

- Don't, if confronted, deny or confirm to other colleagues that you are having an affair. Only when there is cast-iron evidence that the liaison has been damaging to your work or has marred your integrity should you confess.

- Don't look for sympathy or inflict your pain on others when things go wrong. After a very short time, conspicuous distress can be an imposition on people. Sudden deep sighs and copious middle-distance staring is vexatious to others; the best remedies for genuine heartbreak are time and complete absorption in work.

Farewell, my lovely

There is a practical reason why women should avoid workplace sexual relationships. Attitudes to male and female equality have a long way to go in most companies. So if, after an affair has broken up, a male and female manager can't bear the sight of one another across the conference table, the convention is for the company to take the man's side and to let the little lady go. On that basis a female secretary who has come to the end of an affair with her male boss had better start checking the job pages.

How women can avoid affairs

'This isn't the place to talk about what I have on my mind. Let's have a drink together later.' Don't.

But then, most adult women would recognise a crooked pass like that from well behind the touch-line. Turning on the heel and walking off is one way of dealing with it. But an obvious rebuff may not always be the best response. Dealing with the subtle and insidious approach with minimum embarrassment and resentment calls for more skill. To fend off unwanted approaches in tricky circumstances, one of the following techniques, or a combination thereof, may work:

- If invited for social drinks after work, invite – or arrive with – a friend. And don't advertise your independence by staying too long.

- If you are approached by an ardent, hard-to-resist close colleague, the best protection is to put him off with excuses of unalterable obligations – evening classes, drama clubs, cultural societies and so on – every evening and every weekend for a month at least. He may lose interest and turn his attention to other more available prospects. If that doesn't work, keep your excuses going for another month.

- If you are on a diet, doing an exercise course or some other physical improvement regime, don't discuss it with male colleagues. It draws attention to your body and creates a perfect opening for a pass.

- If cornered, talk about a boyfriend, your family, and your remorseless social life.

- If you have no boyfriend, manufacture one – currently on overseas assignment, to whom you are devoted and after whom you pine.

- If you don't wish to make men think they are under starter's orders, don't respond enthusiastically to flattery.

- If you don't want to invite intimacy, don't confide your personal feelings in colleagues of the opposite sex.

If all other rejection techniques fail, try honesty. Explain that your rule is never to mix work and personal relationships. It is a rule you refuse to break under any circumstances. If you get away with that, his ego and your career are not threatened.

The office party

These are a minefield. Rather than risk the dangers, many people simply don't go to them. This is not always a good idea. If you don't like office parties, you should at least make an effort to endure them for a short period. Simply saying that you don't go to them on principle can brand you a snob.

When you go under sufferance, arm yourself with a get-out. Make it known that you can stay for only a short time because you have another long-standing appointment afterwards that can't be cancelled.

Safety first

If a friend offers you a lift home, but is drinking too much, explain that you are making other arrangements; then ensure that someone drives him home.

Don't believe any flattery after the first round of drinks.

Alternative entertainment

To avoid the chance of embarrassment and mortification, an office party can be organised that does not involve over-imbibing and inflammatory physical contact. Perhaps a meal at a good restaurant, including a sensible amount of wine – none for drivers unless lifts and taxis are pre-arranged. Otherwise organise a cabaret or a visit to a theatre followed or preceded by a meal.

Whatever the celebration, restrict the use of cameras to a professional – engaged for his qualities of discretion. And consider prohibiting video-cameras all together. Some people will not appreciate being reminded of their feature role as a paralytic drunk roaming the terrain looking for someone else to interfere with.

Sexual harassment

To those who suffer it, sexual harassment is not a joke. It involves not just conduct of the worst possible kind, but it is also deeply insulting. On the other hand, to allow someone to harass you without trying to stop it demonstrates not tolerance but irresponsibility and ineptitude.

A sign of the nineties is that this section is not aimed entirely at women. Women executives often find male colleagues or staff attractive. The difference is usually that the female is more discerning than the male – she picks off her victim with a rifle shot rather than a scatter gun.

Who . . . me?

Some people, both offender and offended, don't know where harmless flirtation ends and sexual harassment begins. There are borders across which no courteous male or female should stray, the most obvious of which are:

- Touching someone intimately

- Making lascivious remarks to or about someone

- Staring at someone or eyeing them up and down

- Continuing to make advances after having been firmly rejected

- Even in a joke, suggesting someone will be penalised unless he/she submits to one's advances

- Publicly grabbing, slapping, tickling, pinching. Women in particular find such actions deeply insulting

Actual sexual advances

Laws are in place to deal with sexual harassment at work, but one should be alert to the signs of approaching danger and, if possible, deal with them *constructively*. That means without resorting to legal action, getting anyone the sack, or causing a prolonged and disruptive fuss.

This may seem a feeble response to such distressing behaviour, but it is realistic. If you wish to retain a job you otherwise enjoy, revenge should have no place in your strategy.

When countering sexually harassment yourself, you may first need to overcome your embarrassment, particularly when dealing with a person whom you may otherwise respect, or who has some professional power over you. These points may help in that process:

- Explain in private that your fidelity is to someone else and that the situation is causing you distress

- Firmly but politely explain that you find this behaviour totally unacceptable and it has to stop

- Ask the offender to explain his behaviour, as to you it is acutely unpleasant and unappreciated

- Explain that your loyalty to him as your colleague is being endangered

- Add that, although some people may be flattered by attention, you find this harassment intolerable

- If this is not sufficient discouragement, it should be tried again, but this time within earshot of others

- Should that not work, mobilise your colleagues of both sexes; explain what is happening and ask for their help.

- You could try making it the workplace joke. Collective sniggering has a dampening effect on the rampant

- Alternatively, a colleague's warning to the harasser of the dire seriousness of the situation may do the trick

If none of those measures works, you must report the situation to the personnel manager or equivalent, and if necessary take legal action. Your employer may also be liable for prosecution in a sexual harassment case.

Chapter 7

CRITICISM

ACCORDING to the celebrated piece of graffiti, 'Just because I'm paranoid doesn't mean people *aren't* persecuting me.' Criticism can be a potent form of persecution, and just about everyone is affected by it. The opinions of others are important to us, and can have an insidious influence on our mood, attitude and performance.

> Throughout their careers, executives have to cope with criticism – both received and delivered. The keys to mastering it are a genuine understanding of its effects, and compassion for those who suffer it.

Critically wrong

The directors of a well-known British manufacturing company were concerned at the low and deteriorating output at one of their factories. Part of the problem was traced to low company morale. Among the contributory factors was the local manager's practice of posting a large bar chart in the centre of the shop-floor notice board which graphically indicated how the workforce's efforts were failing to reach productivity targets each week. The manager would append comments like 'Full marks for consistency! Figures down for the fourth week in a row' and 'Bottom of the league for productivity *again*.' It made depressing reading and was a significant factor in achieving one particular plant record, that of absenteeism.

. . . And right

A promising young manager in a thriving manufacturing company regularly turned up for work dressed like a B-movie spiv. He had no idea of the odd impression he made on colleagues, superiors and visiting clients. The man was in fact an eccentric thirty-year-old bachelor who actually believed that he dressed with flair.

His boss knew that criticising him for his outfits and revealing that he was a figure of some derision among the younger staff would cause him serious embarrassment. His solution was starkly simple, and above all, constructive. He explained that prospects for promotion to middle management would be improved if he dressed like they did. He made certain recommendations for more appropriate apparel. He also tactfully suggested that his secretary accompany him on a shopping expedition to a store whose more discreet stock best suited their field of business.

Judicious criticism

It doesn't take an expert to criticise. The expertise comes in admonishing someone constructively and without upsetting his self-esteem. The right kind of criticism is never directed at an individual's character but at the way he works.

> Positive criticism doesn't send someone away humiliated and resentful. It motivates him to work better and harder.

The role of the critic

It is worth examining one's own motives before becoming a critic of others. For example, is a particular criticism justified, or does the responsibility lie with someone else's – perhaps your own – ineptitude? Is the criticism work-based or more to do with personal bias? Some incidents may involve both, but you need to recognise the difference and temper your approach accordingly.

If you are about to carpet someone, ask yourself if the admonishment has a positive intent or merely a destructive one.

- When it is positive, decide in advance what you hope to achieve by the criticism

- When it is just destructive, examine your own motives for the onslaught.

If the victim is not to be fired, it is vital to the company that he is given the opportunity and advice that could improve his performance in future. So a reproach should be combined with an offer to help find a solution to improve matters.

A valuable but flawed employee, who lacks certain basic human skills, may benefit from one of the scores of available training courses that range from Customer Service and Communications to Business Etiquette itself.

The critical stage

Unless it is for very good strategic reasons, no one should be criticised in the presence of colleagues. Criticism is a private affair and wherever possible should be delivered discreetly.

Criticism should be meted out piecemeal. Dealing with more than one or two unsatisfactory issues at a time can be manifestly demoralising. Wholesale criticisms should be applied only when accompanied by recommendations for a major shift in strategy.

Nor should criticism be spread too broadly across the company. Complaining to the entire staff for the company's 'poor performance' is unjust, inconsiderate and seriously damaging to morale, particularly if the problem proves to emanate from only one or two inadequate departments.

Critical respect

Whether the criticism is based on personal issues or just on work, the accused must be treated with respect. He must be allowed the chance to reply to all charges. Even though people often suspect their faults themselves, they don't always have the ability or experience to correct them. Of equal importance is the fact that they may not know a face-saving – or job-saving – way of asking for help.

Wherever possible, alternate criticism with acknowledgment of successes. One's purpose is to improve a commercial situation, not to punish as a teacher would a wayward pupil.

Assessment reviews

Some companies hold reviews of personnel performance on a yearly basis. Where this is considered too long an interval, an open-door policy should be instituted so problems can be aired and dealt with in good time. The best kind of improvements can be achieved when staff are self-motivated. Discussing problems with employees as they occur, and steering them towards suggesting their own solutions, is an adroit and effective technique. Their job experience makes them the best qualified to apply practical answers to specific problems.

It is a wise boss who ignores the occasional petty problems that do not affect his employees' welfare or the company's productivity.

Booby traps

- Resentment against the organisation could be simmering along with poor performance. Before criticising, invite complaints about any lack of support an employee suffers in the company. If they are justified, your criticism may not be

- Watch out for your own idiosyncrasies. If, for instance, you are irritated by people shouting across the office, that doesn't necessarily make it a major offence

- Try not to criticise when you are tired or stressed – your judgment will be impaired

- When criticism for a serious issue is thoroughly merited, it should be delivered in a straightforward manner. Be careful that your own depth of feeling about the matter is communicated without venom

- At all costs avoid sarcasm or ridiculing people – these practices are contagious and they damage morale

- Beware of criticising an individual employee for a general weakness among the staff

- Avoid the temptation to demonstrate to an established employee how his job should be done. It may make him feel small and arouse rancour.

'When you have to point out someone's blunder, it is in no one's interests – not yours, not the blunderer's and certainly not your company's – just to let off a fierce head of steam. That's demoralising and immobilising. If you're looking for a positive outcome, you have to remember that criticism is a creative process.'

LEN FLETCHER, Sales and Marketing Director of Pitney-Bowes.

Bad news

News such as dismissal should always be delivered in private, giving the casualty the chance to react normally without fear of being observed by others.

When you have to tell staff about cutbacks, redundancies or other such negative issues, do not delegate the responsibility to someone else. Prepare yourself properly for the task, with the welfare of those affected as your paramount concern.

Dismissal

When you *must* dismiss someone, you are not entitled to criticise him for anything other than his lack of job performance. His demeanour may not show it, but his confidence will have taken a blow, so be sensitive to piling on too long a list of reasons for his rejection. But be sure he understands clearly why he is being 'let go'. Short of hypocrisy, and regardless of how much you consider the person deserves his fate, you should demonstrate a compassionate attitude.

Always follow a sacking with encouragement. Explain that, in your view, the person's abilities may be better suited to another occupation. If possible, suggest employment sources or companies that he might try. Encourage him to think about future possibilities. Tell him that, should he require a reference from you, you will be sure to include his good points.

When taking someone's job away, it is the boss's responsibility to ensure they are left with their dignity intact.

Accepting criticism

The platitude 'I don't mind criticism, so long as it's constructive' is hard to believe. Most people have a serious aversion to being censured. Understandably so, as criticism is the converse of praise, and in business it is not career-enhancing.

But, accepting that criticism will not make you feel good, there are ways of accepting it positively and with commendable grace. First, one must recognise that when criticism is sensible and justified it is aimed not at the person, but at the performance. Indeed, positive criticism delivered by an experienced and sensitive boss may provoke a change of course that will prove beneficial.

'Every one of us reacts differently to criticism. Even a person's gender is a factor. For example, women often form close friendships with their business colleagues, but that can make it difficult for them to accept criticism from one another. Men have their own problems, frequently to do with more fragile egos. It's a minefield.'

LOIS JACOBS, Managing Director of HP:ICM, one of Europe's leading business communications companies.

Listen!

Even if you consider a piece of criticism to be unjustified, don't respond with a stream of rebuttals. Listen carefully to the reprimand before reacting. If you are criticised in the presence of other people, stay cool, explain to your accuser that you don't think this is the appropriate time or place to discuss the issue, and that you would like to see him in his office to discuss it fully.

The professional reaction

When looking to move people up the promotion ladder, trained senior managers often take special note of the way people react to criticism. The qualities they seek are the ability to take criticism seriously, while remaining pleasant and open-minded and then proving that one learns from one's mistakes.

Should your boss consider you are in the wrong, the worst thing you can do is shrug off his reprimand. Explain your thinking, then ask him for suggestions to minimise any damage or to improve performance in that particular area. Finally, even if it makes your gums bleed, thank him for offering the criticism and for indicating a just resolution.

Justified criticism

If the charges are justified, explain that you would like time to consider them carefully before pleading guilty. There may be mitigating factors and even credit to salvage if you can prove that, despite mistakes being made, you used initiative and were well motivated.

Unjustified criticism

If you consider you are being unjustifiably criticised to your boss by someone within your department, restrain your wish to remonstrate. Ask for the source of the complaint and, without attacking the character or integrity of the accuser, justify your position in terms of its purpose if not its outcome.

Try not to over-react to unfair criticism. Explain that you will review the situation and bring about any changes that are necessary, but that if the charges turn out to be unjustified you would like the opportunity to discuss the matter further.

Remember to control your temper if you are unjustly charged. Someone might be trying to achieve just that reaction. It will be very much to your credit if you maintain your dignity throughout the ordeal.

If you are subject to constant and unfair criticism, either change your job or go the whole hog and organise a management buyout.

Chapter 8

HOT TOPICS – RUMOUR, GOSSIP, SMOKING, PUNCTUALITY AND PRIVATE LIFE

R UMOUR and gossip are the adulterated spice of the working day, sometimes bland, usually negative, often unwholesome. But (between you and me) tapping into such transmissions may occasionally be in a manager's interests, as they can incorporate useful commercial information. On the other hand, when gossip and rumour are malicious and destructive they can harm careers, business relationships and the company itself.

Equally contentious is the issue of smoking, a practice that is widely resented and increasingly regulated in business life. The conflict has been exacerbated by revelations of the dangers of passive smoking: medical authorities now maintain that smoking is even more harmful to those who are forced to breathe in the emissions from others' cigarettes/cigars/pipes.

And, better late than not at all, we discuss the issue of punctuality, closely followed by private life.

Rumour control

The fastest-moving of workplace rumours are those concerned with mergers and takeovers. They regularly outstrip official memos and often provide a middle manager's first indication of important corporate manoeuvres. But such scuttlebuck can be damaging to company morale. So it is a manager's moral obligation to discover the facts and enlighten his staff as soon as possible.

If the rumours are false, they must be repudiated at once. However, if they are essentially true and could mean redundancies, there is little that can be done to suppress them – in advance of an official announcement –

without making matters worse. So a diplomatic silence is the wisest policy.

Gossip

Regulating damaging gossip

Much workplace gossip is concerned with the connection between working practices and personal relationships; in a word, favouritism. The solution is not to attempt to suppress the chatter, because that would merely allow resentments to simmer. If the charges are baseless, the manager should supervise a civilised meeting between the protagonists and clear the air.

> However reluctant a manager may be to march into quicksand, he must recognise that unjustified and personally directed gossip will harm morale, working practices and productivity.

Unsubstantiated gossip

If gossip is directed at a certain individual, and is unsubstantiated, then it is up to the manager to confront the originator. He should be advised, for the good of the company, to discuss it face-to-face with the injured party. If he refuses, the manager can suggest to the victim that he takes the initiative and confronts the originator of the stories. Having done so, the injured party will have a tactical advantage in debate and a better psychological platform on which to conduct his case with courtesy and firmness.

The manager can suggest that the victim questions his accuser on the following lines: 'I'm very upset that you are involved in spreading stories about me. Can you repeat them to my face? Do you have any evidence of what you are saying about me? Where did you get this so-called information?'

The victim should offer his explanation. If the story is thus seen to be unfounded, all those involved in it should be invited to apologise, privately or otherwise. This should be followed by a statutory halt to all verbal hostilities. The manager should explain to those concerned that their ability to work together is seriously affected by malevolent gossip, and that, if it occurs again, for the good of the company the contestants will be separated, even if it means dismissals.

> Malicious gossip must be firmly handled, and all the life squeezed out of it. Failure to do so may mean that the combatants remain lifetime enemies and their working performance will suffer.

Substantiated gossip

The manager can handle harmful gossip directly by taking the originator of the story to one side and explaining that the talk is upsetting business. Should the originator maintain that the problem is not the gossip but the issue – be it a disruptive relationship or someone's job ability – then the manager must interview the accused and take the matter into his own hands.

Smoking

This contentious issue is clouded with hypocrisy from both addicts and opponents. Smokers are told, ad nauseam, that smoking makes rooms dirty, smelly and untidy, that it infects clothes, handbags and hair, contaminates breath, stains teeth and hands and is the root of ugly coughs. Not to mention that – according to a report published in 1990 by the Royal College of Physicians – it kills three hundred people a day in the UK. More alarmingly perhaps, they say that six non-smokers a day die from passively inhaling the fumes from others' cigarettes. Quite an indictment, so little wonder that most smokers are guilt-ridden.

This damning evidence makes many opponents of smoking angry, resentful, sanctimonious, discourteous and unsympathetic to the smoker's pitiful plight. That's a harsh position when, after all, no one *wants* to be addicted to smoking.

No-smoking areas

If the majority, or a vehement minority, of employees do not wish to suffer the disagreeable fall-out from cigarettes, or object to running the risks of passive smoking, they should be entitled to ask for the practice to be prohibited in their working area. For the smokers to object to such a ban would be inconsiderate and selfish. Furthermore, it can be illegal to inflict cigarette smoke on others; an asthmatic was recently awarded compensation in a court of law, because she had been forced to endure passive smoking.

The prevalent thinking on smoking at many offices and plants is that those who smoke should have a specific and separate area in which to do so. Out of consideration for the addicts, people should try not to make facetious or critical remarks about the area and those who frequent it. The incumbents feel badly enough already.

For smoking in meetings see page 70.

The rules of combustion

When a smoker and a non-smoker get together, the former should refrain from smoking. Even if he seeks and is granted permission, he is imposing on the other's good nature, professional position and health.

Smoking in the street is not good manners. It is also unsightly and unbecoming.

It is impolite to smoke when other people are eating, including at neighbouring tables. It is implicitly impolite to have the gall to ask if people mind if you smoke while they eat.

Cigarettes burn a large hole in some people's budget, so you should not accept them without reciprocating. And those who do not carry cigarettes ('I'm trying to give them up' etc.) but smoke other people's, will not win anyone's popularity contests.

Cigars and pipes

With their greater noxious range, cigar and pipe smokers should consider the welfare of an even wider circle. So potent is the aroma of a cigar or pipe tobacco that it impinges on the comfort of everyone in the same room. If in any doubt of its effect on others, the obvious rule is not to light up.

When armed with cigars, in smoking company, ensure you have a sufficient number to hand around. If you don't have enough for the others, rather than apologise you should refrain altogether.

Ashtrays

Whether at work or in a restaurant, the ashtray should be kept close to you and well away from consenting non-smokers. Ash should be kept at a low level, so there is no risk of it being scattered around, or of the ashtray capsizing over furniture or carpets.

If no ashtrays are evident, whether in a workplace or at someone's home, permission should be asked to smoke only as a last resort. Their absence could indicate policy or attitude.

Smokers have a personal responsibility for their ashtrays. They should empty them themselves, before leaving their workplace or someone's home.

Punctuality

Having to wait for late-comers shortens tempers, extends resentment and causes inconvenience and offence.

Walking in on people ahead of time isn't always a good idea either. Managers who, without good reason, descend early on subordinates may be considered haughty and arrogant. It can interrupt people's work, disrupt their schedule and inconvenience those with prior claims on their time. The same principle governs anyone who takes advantage of his superior position to disregard appointments with those who have to grin and bear it.

Timing excuses

If you are anticipating arriving either significantly early or late, the form is to ring through as well in advance as possible.

When someone turns up late for an appointment, those kept waiting are rarely satisfied when it is simply blamed on traffic (other than the flying kind). There is the feeling that those who do not take into account possible rail delays and road snarl-ups have yet to arrive in the 1990s.

However entertaining the excuse when late, the others rarely smile from the heart. Amusement and sympathy are often superficial; resentment may ferment under the surface . . . along with a feeling of being personally slighted. The only possible antidote for this cocktail of bruised emotions is for excuses and apologies to be proffered seriously and sincerely on entry, and again at the end of the meeting.

There are other good, tactical reasons not to be late for a meeting:

- It puts you at a disadvantage because you don't have time to gather your thoughts properly

- You may not recognise the pecking order

- It is difficult to merge into the established ambience

- You will not know if the contribution you wish to make has already been covered or, worse still, discarded.

Static punctuality

Extra care and succour are required for someone who arrives punctually for an appointment with you, but has to be kept waiting. It is important to show both your respect for the guest and the wish to mollify any inconvenience.

Where humanly possible, extricate yourself temporarily from your urgent task in order personally to make your excuses. Failing that, an assistant or secretary should do so on your behalf, with a personal message from you. This should not merely be a cursory 'He won't keep you waiting too long'; it should be a more solicitous 'He knows you are here, and he is very sorry for keeping you waiting. He is doing his best not to delay you more than absolutely necessary.'

The guest should be provided with refreshment (wherever possible not in a paper cup but in the good old-fashioned cup and saucer format), and offered magazines or other literature. His reading should be regularly interrupted with polite updates on your approaching availability.

If, after twenty minutes, you can still see no imminent prospect of fulfilling the appointment, come out and personally explain the situation. Offer him the option of another date and make whatever concession possible in terms of time and perhaps location. Do not leave it at that. Whether you see him after a serious delay or the appointment has to be postponed, you must send an apology, or include one in your next letter to him. It is good manners to comment regretfully on the incident at your next meeting.

However much he may protest that no damage has been done, there is no denying that you have wasted his time, cost him money and taxed his goodwill. Long-term rancour will be averted if you demonstrate that you appreciate the damage done and demonstrate your wish to make up for the trouble caused.

Punctuality at work

> When an employee replies to the question 'Why weren't you here at 9am, Jones?' with the answer 'Why, what happened?', you know that their attitude to punctuality is adrift.

An employee is paid for work done within certain time limits and it is up to him to fulfil that function. If he continually arrives late, his manager should discuss with him his work and domestic circumstances, and the situation should be remedied in as realistic and sympathetic a manner as possible.

Everyone in a company should realise that it is inadmissible to be constantly late for work. It is also a breach of contract and trust.

If the transport situation means that someone has the choice of arriving either forty-five minutes early or fifteen minutes late, and the latter make more sense, then it is realistic to ask him to make up for it by working the lost time in his lunch hour or in the evening. If that isn't practical, then an early start, with breakfast at a nearby café, may be the only solution.

Private life clashes

To some people, work is something they do in the intervals between 'real life'. But that does not stop them from shortening those intervals as much as possible with doctor's, dentist's and hairdresser's appointments, or by nipping off early for a dinner or theatre date. To some other people, home and social activities are crammed into the intervals between 'real life' which they believe happens at work.

Between these two groups – the workoholics and the time-fillers – are the more reasonable types with a more balanced view on the subject, but who still, on occasions, have trouble sorting out the priorities.

So when business and personal life clash – for example, when an employee wants to get away early for a curtain-up – he should give his manager as much notice as possible and not request permission on the same day. When a good and fair working relationship is established, a manager will not unreasonably deny an early exit. In his turn, the employee should volunteer to come in early in the morning to make up for the time lost.

When a medical appointment is on the cards, one should try wherever possible to make it on the way to or from work, in a lunch hour or on a Saturday, but never in the heart of the business day.

'The practice of good business etiquette enables your brain to relate at all levels most effectively with other people. When you use the appropriate etiquette your capability is expanded, your memory improves, your communication is better, your stress levels are reduced and you are instantaneously more popular, happy and successful.'

TONY BUZAN, advisor to governments and multinational organisations, and TV presenter, lecturer, writer and producer, and former editor of the *International Journal of MENSA*.

Chapter 9
====

MEETINGS

A COMMERCIAL consultant once calculated that each year about 50 billion business meetings are held around the world. Among the extrapolations from this estimate are that some 35 billion are routine, 10 billion pointless and 5 billion counter-productive. Of them, 48 billion are said to be worthwhile, of which fewer than 24 billion probably are.

What is unarguable is that a considerable proportion of all meetings are the settings for responsibility-shifting, power plays and sub-veneer dissidence. All of these are the dry tinder of incivility.

A code of conduct in the organising and running of meetings can help to ease tensions, improve relationships and even create amiable and fertile foundations for shared benefit – which is what the 50 billion meetings a year are supposed to be about in the first place.

'If you need to have a meeting you are probably fudging an issue.'

PETER GUMMER, Chairman of Shandwick plc, the world's largest public relations consultancy.

Knowhow for fixing meetings

It is a sage and considerate businessman who ensures that appointments for meetings are not just made, but arranged. Where possible, the time and location of external appointments should be coordinated to suit not only the convenor or senior person but the majority of the gathering.

Mornings are normally the best times for meetings; people are fresher, and decisions arising may be implemented in the course of the day. Friday afternoons are not a good time, as many people have begun to wind down for the weekend.

When drawing up the list of participants, the line should be carefully negotiated between inviting everyone who could successfully contribute and those who would be dead wood. Consideration should be paid to sending courtesy invitations to non-participating observers.

Agendas should, if possible, be sent with the notification, enabling people to prepare themselves and the necessary material. Preparation is a key element for all meetings.

> 'A one hour meeting for eight people takes a one-man day. Being ill-prepared not only wastes time, it is the height of ill manners. . . .'
>
> PETER GUMMER, Chairman of Shandwick plc.

In some circumstances, it is worthwhile to ask participants if they would like to bring any special equipment such as slides, videotapes, graphic materials and so on. Should they require hardware, technical aids, and so on, system formats should be verified.

Ideally, the time of the meeting should include a contingency period of fifteen minutes in case of over-running. Adequate time should be built in for delays when people are travelling from overseas or from particularly long distances.

Easy-access meetings should be scheduled for as short a duration as possible. This will be appreciated by busy people; it helps to apply the mind to the subject in question as well as to inhibit the flow of red herrings.

On receipt of the notification, outside participants should immediately either write to indicate their acceptance or telephone to request alternative dates. Where someone can attend but will have to leave early, he should ask in advance for the agenda to be adjusted accordingly.

In advance designate someone to take minutes of the meeting, if they are required, rather than waste the first five minutes of the meeting deciding who's going to do it.

Ambient considerations

The room should be adequately large to accommodate everyone comfortably, but not so large as to suggest one has had to extemporise. The room's condition, facilities and equipment should be checked before the meeting, allowing time for emergency measures, upgrading and airing.

Profuse coffee (including de-caffeinated), tea, mineral water and/or fruit juice should be available. These are not an indulgence: they sustain people and help to relax the atmosphere. The person hosting the meeting should delegate someone to serve the first 'round'. Thereafter everyone can be asked to help themselves, with the host ensuring that they do so.

People should be given elbow room, but should observe territorial imperatives by not spreading their papers into others' space. Every place should have its own writing instrument and pad; waste bins should be conveniently placed.

If the rule is no smoking, a sign should be placed on the outside door or on the wall, and no ashtrays should be in evidence. An outside area should be designated for those who wish to smoke during a break. If people will definitely be smoking, enough ashtrays should be provided to prevent people having to stretch-and-share.

Pre-meeting checklist:

- Are there enough chairs (count number)?
- Are technical aids (e.g. overhead projector) set up?
- Have sufficient pens and pads been laid out (count number)?
- Have waste bins been provided?
- Are there sufficient ashtrays (if required)?
- Has liquid refreshment been laid on?
- Have arrangements been made for someone to take calls?
- Has someone been designated to take minutes?

Opening meetings

People sometimes arrive at meetings in ascending order of seniority, which is more psychology than gentility.

Junior participants should wait until others have chosen their seats before sitting down. Visitors should enquire about seating protocol before they do so. People should sit down on arrival; if they are visitors to the company they should stand when its most senior executives enter, in which case, even if it is not company protocol, the others should follow suit.

It is good form never to arrive after the person who is to chair the meeting. In an ideal world he arrives last, bang on time, and starts the meeting immediately. The chairman should take responsibility for all introductions. They should be as full as time permits, but, around a large table, orchestrated so as to avoid prolific handshaking. No matter how informal the meeting, the chairman should have prepared a few opening words to kick it off.

The good, the bad and the boorish

Remember the celebrated adage 'It is dangerous to win arguments at business meetings. You gain a point at the cost of your opponents' goodwill.' That is just one indication of the complexities of such assemblies. Business meetings can be vicious and ruthless – but both short-term advantage and long-term benefits come to those who maintain composure and display respect for every individual present.

A knowledge of good business etiquette at meetings gives a person manifest self-confidence as well as an edge on those who behave insensitively.

Uncultivated behaviour can be revealing. It exposes:

- Who is garrulous, but ill-informed
- Who is well-informed but a poor communicator
- Who is dynamic but emotionally driven
- Who has integrity and who may be treacherous.

All this is demonstrated through their attitude to others. Such people will display a number of self-defeating characteristics:

- They will interrupt people, indicating that what they have to say is more important
- They will display boredom or irritation
- They will be offensive, perhaps using personal knowledge to belittle someone
- They will run their own cabals while others are speaking
- They will make private jokes
- They will patronise their subordinates
- They will lose their tempers and raise their voices
- They will become visibly frustrated when interrupted
- They will behave sycophantically to the chairman and other seniors

Well-mannered delegates, on the other hand, will not only avoid, or at least tactically control all such behaviour, but will also display other positive characteristics:

- They will listen carefully, giving the speaker the time to make his case in full

- They will not interrupt or interject except through the chairman

- They will not waste people's time with trivial or irrelevant questions

- They will draw attention to themselves only if they have sensible ideas, modifications, or solutions to a problem

- They will speak firmly and when interrupted will ask politely, just once, to be allowed to finish. Ultimately they will never take the undignified paths of trying to out-talk, brow-beat or shout anyone down.

Meeting minefields

When first presenting a new idea one should present the fundamentals, not the finished product. In this way, you do not impose on others' territory, and you elicit enthusiasm not nit-picking.

When attacked on an issue not relevant to the meeting, do not defend yourself. It is demeaning to you and embarrassing for the assembly. Tell the attacker firmly that this is neither the place nor time for such a discussion, but that you would very much like to debate the issue in full after the meeting.

When you are required on the phone, try to avoid taking the call. If it really is important, excuse yourself quietly to the chairman and leave and return unobtrusively, knowing that you have made a tactically damaging move and may have left yourself vulnerable. There are worse things done at meetings: taking a portable telephone in is one of them (see Chapter 4).

Chairman's etiquette

If the guest list has been carefully drafted, everyone will have something valuable to contribute. The chairman of the meeting should ensure that they all have the chance to speak. No one, including the chairman, should monopolise the meeting. Notwithstanding a person's talent, track record and enthusiasm, without proper management he may inhibit others' contributions. A good chairman will control such a person's ardour with tact and respect, without damage to anyone's self-esteem.

The chairman will be under constant scrutiny. His attitudes and reactions will be closely observed throughout the meeting. He should therefore sit up straight and his demeanour should be alert and positive.

Meetings are frequently arduous, and the chairman is responsible to the other participants for not allowing people to stray from the subject, ride their hobby horses or otherwise waste time. At the end he should summarise the meeting, and then offer everyone the opportunity to comment on and amend his conclusion. The closing essential is for the chairman to thank all present for attending.

Chapter 10

CONFERENCES, EXHIBITIONS AND TRADE FAIRS

A S conferences, exhibitions and fairs are invariably staged out of the ordinary working environment, they seem to induce out-of-the-ordinary behaviour from the unfettered corporate body.

A production company will organise a conference or exhibition along with the entertainment and other activities, but they have no obligation to control your delegates' conduct. It is the client company's responsibility to protect its own reputation, and to prevent business relationships from being washed up on the shores of distant business locations.

The elements of playing away from home: staying in hotels, eating out, renewing old relationships, developing new ones, and being separated from the discipline of business and family routines – all this creates the need for a code of behaviour to be established well in advance of the event.

Managing discipline

One method of maintaining proper discipline at company conferences or exhibitions is to make divisional or departmental managers responsible for the conduct of their own people. They should liaise with the other managers, under the general supervision of the company executive in charge of administration.

Each manager should be charged with briefing his department on an agreed code of behaviour. In so doing, he may wish to remind them of the damage that can be inflicted on the company by such factors as late night noise, drinking in large groups and to excess, and behaving disrepectfully to women and to staff. He should certainly emphasise that the delegates are representing their company at all times and that its reputation must be upheld.

In collaboration with the conference organisers, managers can also be made responsible for organising gratuities and possibly presents for hotel and exhibition hall staff, to express appreciation from their particular group and to leave an enduring good image for the company.

Conference bracer

Whatever the tactics governing the audiences at such gatherings, the presenters and speechmakers themselves cannot afford to relax, at least not until their primary task is discharged.

All speakers should be properly coached and thoroughly rehearsed in their presentations. (An important consideration, this; the audience is entitled to good speeches from everyone, not just the top speakers.) Speakers should be aware of their alloted time and avoid overrunning.

Presenters should be advised on one cardinal rule of conference speaking: that drinking alcohol beforehand can be perilously counterproductive. In a stressful conference environment, drinking is certainly not a reliable tranquilliser. It speeds the metabolic rate, increases adrenalin secretion and makes one careless. Furthermore, under the pressure of making a presentation before an important audience, drink has a more potent effect than normal. Although the presenter himself may not be aware of the full impact of drink, the audience will quickly detect speech slurs, awkward gestures, increased blink rate and a flushed countenance.

Spouses

If spouses accompany delegates, it is considerate to organise trips and outings for them while the business conference is in progress. As interests vary, and a duvet-stuffing demonstration may not interest a devotee of kick-wrestling, there should be a choice. To please most of the people most of the time, it is best to stick to such activities as lectures and outings based on local highlights, colourful and animated cultural performances, and, sometimes, sporting occasions.

Although these outings should be voluntary, it is unwise for spouses to spend all the time lying under the ozone-free blue skies, rumbling in the jacuzzi and eating meals in their room. A company grapevine quickly pulsates with stories of snootiness and unsociability. Spouses are invited along for social reasons. Conferences are not free-for-all, no-strings-attached holidays. If partners are not prepared to join in, they should think seriously about making their excuses and not going.

Pairing

Conference settings can be very romantic; they can also be the location for troublesome sexual scandals and jealousies (see Chapter 6). If a delegate wishes to bring someone who is not his long-term partner, separate rooms should be booked (the delegate should pay the supplement) even if only one is used. Hypocritical yes, but prudent.

Playing away slackens inhibitions, with room-hopping a feature event. The professionally ambitious do so at their peril – as does anyone, single or otherwise. Repercussions may have to be faced and normal business relationships resumed when one lands back at work.

Exhibiting strain

By their very nature, exhibitions are organised and promoted as stimulating events. But behind the facades they can be tough on stand staff who suffer the creeping paralysis that starts at the soles of the feet, creeps along the ankles, upward through the back, up the neck and into the brain.

Many people find exhibitions exhausting, unhealthy (most artificial heating and cooling systems are mentally and physically debilitating), repetitive and tedious. And yet their performance is central to the success of the enterprise. So it is in the interests of the company exhibiting, the exhibition organisers, the customers and the staff, to make the experience as endurable and enjoyable as possible.

Staffing levels

People's proficiency, it is scientifically claimed, drops markedly after a two-hour stretch. During days of unremitting pressure, organising timetables and breaks on this basis will help maintain enthusiasm and effectiveness.

'Numbers' is always a difficult game at exhibitions. One cannot easily anticipate busy or slack periods. An effective way of avoiding stress is to create efficient and compatible teams. The combination not only lessens the austerity of the experience, but also increases the pleasure of the staff; and when the staff feel good the allure of the stand is increased.

Soft sell

The British are still not comfortable when being subjected to the hard sell. They can be upset easily when physically waylaid and herded on to a stand. Over-forceful techniques by staff may give the company a hassling, market-trader image. Aside from display and merchandising tactics, the most effective way of encouraging people to visit your stand is through the relaxed and friendly attitudes of your staff.

> 'A key point in selling or any business discipline, is building and maintaining a good impression. Correct social behaviour and first class inter-personal skills are as important today as formal skills, particularly with the new order of trade within Europe and the world.'
>
> BARRIE LOCK, Managing Director of Plan 2000, a leading sales training company.

Browsers

If you are exhibiting near a railway station or airport, beware of cancellations. It may let loose a train- or plane-full of deposed passengers with nothing else to do but to kill some time – yours as well as theirs.

However, those who man the stand should appreciate that everyone is a potential customer or opinion influencer. People never forget those who are rude to them. One day in the future, a browser who was given short shrift by your staff may be in a position to return the gesture by doing business with your competitors.

The civil and practical approach is to arm obvious casual visitors with literature to read at their leisure, explaining truthfully that to cover the entire topic on the spot would take up an undue amount of their time.

> The staff's courteous treatment of all-comers on an exhibition stand is an observable corporate plus. Treating anyone in a rude and off-hand manner not only discredits the company but generates a generally bad and mercenary atmosphere on the stand.

Spy alert

Other time-wasters may be your competitors, purloining corporate intelligence. Fortunately, they often show investigative talents on the level of Inspector Clouseau, such as being unable to resist revealing their knowledge about your mutual sphere of operation or asking questions that are conspicuously pointed.

Their presence is unwelcome, of course, but the temptation to frog-march them from the stand should be resisted. A simple and benign solution is to ask for their business card – so they can be sent more information. If they claim not to have a card they should be asked for their address, so that something can be sent on to them. One should never be rude; equally, one should never be duped.

Hospitality

Making alcohol freely available on the stand may be asking for trouble. Far better to have a high-quality private store placed discreetly behind the scenes for special customers. For everyone else, have on offer mineral water and other cool drinks, and if possible coffee (including de-caffeinated) and tea (including herbal).

Staff welfare

The staff will be encouraged and revitalised by a visit from the managing director or head of department. But it is potently counter-productive if the visit is used as a platform for a personal crusade – 'Haven't you unloaded last year's company reports yet?' – or for chivvy-ing everyone along – 'Right, let's all move up a gear' – when they have been in fifth since they started.

Finally, staff should be encouraged not to exchange hot glances with those on other stands. They are inclined to get fanned into torrid affairs.

Chapter 11

CUSTOMER SERVICE AND COMPLAINTS

IN THIS chapter the term 'customer' is taken to mean not only someone from outside the company, but also someone from another
department within the same company. The saying 'The customer is
always right' is wrong, or at least, incomplete. Perhaps it should be:
'The customer should always be *treated* as if he is right.' Someone who
complains should always be treated as if he had suffered material loss or
had been inconvenienced or offended – until it is proved otherwise. In
this way, even those with a tendency to find fault in everyone but themselves, and who do so loudly and aggressively, can effectively be paci-
fied and their belligerence ultimately turned to allegiance.

All it takes is confidence, professionalism and relentless good manners. It is well worth the effort, because the *way* in which complaints are
handled can be as important as the resolution itself.

Attention

A customer who complains can be like an explosive awaiting deto-
nation. He should be handled with care. To respond to his complaints
in a contentious, off-hand, patronising or otherwise negative fashion
serves only to prime his fuse.

> 'As a race the British are reluctant complainers, and perhaps in the
> past that has enabled many businesses to get away with supplying
> a poor level of customer service. This attitude has changed drama-
> tically in recent years. Training people to supply high standards of
> customer service is now a corporate priority.'
>
> SAM WHITBREAD, Chairman of Whitbread & Co plc.

The first rule in defusing a complaint is to *listen*, to give your full attention, then politely to ask questions and review the position so the complainer recognises that his problem is fully understood and taken seriously. Good manners dictate that he should be dealt with as an individual, that is, addressed by name and made to feel he is respected.

The negative reaction

When someone complains, he may be expressing two issues:

- first, the actual complaint
- second, the fact that he has not received due consideration and esteem.

So his ego may be injured.

Consequently, whether dealing with customers or colleagues, the situation will be inflamed if one gives the impression that it is a petty matter, that having to deal with it is a lot of trouble and that really he is a bit of a nuisance. Cold, sarcastic, strident or belittling behaviour will wreck constructive communication and breed ill-will.

The positive approach

Having listened attentively to a complaint, the person handling it should start off by demonstrating an entirely constructive point of view and a willingness to find a solution that satisfies the customer. In this context, it is worth remembering the following points:

- First impressions have a crucial influence on the complainer's attitude
- When face to face with the complainer, friendly eye contact, an alert posture and a pleasant expression will create a conciliatory atmosphere
- One should be seen to regard any reasonable complaint as an opportunity to change a deficient product or process
- The customer should be assured that his complaint is important because it may help to identify and ultimately to rectify any defects in company procedures
- He should be thanked for pointing out a perceived fault – but without admitting any deficiency unless it is proved

- If a complaint is ultimately found to be unjustified, and was made without malice, the complainer should be allowed to withdraw with his dignity intact. ('I'm pleased we managed to sort it all out.')

Delays

Although they may sometimes seem part of the inevitable daily grind to an employee, delays can be infuriating for customers. If someone has had to wait for a long time in a queue or on the phone, one should always apologise to them for the inconvenience caused. It doesn't matter whose fault it is.

> Whoever communicates with the customer represents his company or department, and is at that time individually responsible for good customer relations.

Higher authority

If a problem cannot be resolved or anger de-fused, senior employees should be on hand to help. It is worthwhile establishing an ascending line of communication to cope with such eventualities. A willingness to connect the complainer to someone higher up the ladder demonstrates respect and, of itself, can help take a little of the steam out of an issue. But one should be wary of appearing to pass the buck, and should make sure the procedure has been approved by senior staff. If not they may consider you incapable of handling particular situations yourself.

Defensive fobbing and bouncing

If a complaint comes into the wrong department (see also p. 30), the call should never simply be bounced back to the operator and abandoned. Whoever takes the call should take personal responsibility for ensuring that contact is made with the right person. Meanwhile, the caller should not be kept holding on for a long time without being told what is happening and apologies proffered.

If the correct contact cannot be made at once, the caller's number should be taken so his call can be returned. He should also be given the name and extension number of whoever is handling the call, so he does not feel he is being fobbed off.

A complainer ought not be told to call back. It is the company's responsibility to implement all actions necessary to resolve a problem that the caller considers is their fault.

> 'The rule of thumb is that for every one person who complains to a business there are another ten who are unhappy with the service but don't bother to complain.'
>
> ALAN J. FROST, Managing Director of Abbey Life.

'Oh, no! Not them again'

Criticising your own company or department to an outsider is a virulent practice.

No one should admit guilt on behalf of someone else. Even if a flood of complaints have been made about a particular aspect of his company's or department's performance, an employee should never exacerbate the situation by endorsing it.

Employees should accept that, by taking employment in an organisation, they share credit for its virtues and responsibility for its weaknesses. Their duty, where possible, is to try to alleviate them, even if that is limited to a public relations exercise – handling complaints politely and bringing them to the notice of the appropriate people. When complaints are made, staff loyalty is paramount; not to mention that it is a quality common to successful companies.

Breaking off

There comes a point where a complaining customer may become so belligerent and insulting that he is impossible for inexperienced staff to handle. Employees should be given leave to terminate such conversations with a phrase like 'I'm sorry – you are being offensive, and that won't solve anything. I must ring off.' They shouldn't, however, hang up without warning. Having done so, they should report the incident to a superior and any ensuing onslaught should be passed directly to him.

Written complaints (see also Chapter 5)

If a company does not have a customer relations department, grievances by letter are best handled at the most senior level possible. The complainer may fill his letter with insults and innuendos; these should be rebutted if necesary, but never reciprocated.

Even if a complaint appears at first to be entirely without foundation, it is in everyone's interests to have it investigated thoroughly and then for a reply to be made in full. If a complaint is justified and material injury caused, aside from the statutory recompense, corporate and personal apologies should be expressed – again, from as senior a level as possible, and as promptly as possible.

Handling internal complaints (see also Chapter 7)

Disruption and under-performance are sometimes the result of disputes and poor communication between departments or members of staff. Where one person is clearly at fault, it might be because of problems unrelated to the company. Domestic difficulties may be at the root of his quarrelsome or surly behaviour to colleagues. In this case the situation can be handled confidentially by the department or personnel manager, who may advise the person to seek professional – perhaps legal or medical – help.

A well-tried procedure in one-to-one disputes gives the responsibility for settlement to the department manager. The technique works as follows:

- The manager should be fully briefed as to their substance, and his office – as neutral ground – used for an off-the-record three-way discussion

- First the manager should state objectively the undisputed facts of the case, and obtain agreement about what is true

- Each employee should be given a short period to state his case without interruption by the other

- Where differences of interpretation arise, it is the manager's task to question both employees to try to achieve a consensus

- Should complete contradictions or arguments of fact arise, they may have to be referred to other managers and personnel for verification or denial

- The manager should then suggest a remedy – ideally, one which does not hurt the pride of either party

- If the individuals themselves are able to continue with a satisfactory working relationship, that should be the end of the matter with no disciplinary action needed other than a firm warning against further hostile outbreaks

- In the event of the issue being unresolved, consideration should be given to moving one or both employees (see also p. 58).

How to complain

The most effective, not to say courteous, way of complaining is to focus on the unacceptable service or product and not to criticise the person handling the complaint.

When people feel aggrieved they are often tempted to behave aggressively, and that can be counter-productive. But acting in a way that expresses acquiescence may be equally ineffectual.

Self-assertiveness is the most persuasive attitude. Unlike aggression, it incorporates mutual respect and understanding for the other's problems. A confident, assertive person does not need to use inflammatory language to achieve his aims. He calmly, clearly and politely states his case, without threatening the other person's self-esteem.

Complaining properly ends, as do all successful transactions, with benefits going to both sides.

'Barclays' management and support departments consider front-line sales staff as *their* customers. If our service to them is lacking, then service to the bank's customers is weakened. This internal customer service philosophy is so important that service-contracts are now being drawn up between various departments of the bank itself.'

DAVID CUNNINGHAM, Head of Management Training for Barclays Bank plc.

Part II

SOCIAL SKILLS

Chapter 12

THE BUSINESS LUNCH

BUSINESS lunches are a medley of art forms: the harmonisation of guest and restaurant, the composition of food and drink, the augmentation of stimulating and fruitful conversation, and the amplification of business. At their best, they are agreeable and gratifying. At their worst, they are tedious and time-wasting. A mastery of business lunching – as host, hostess or guest – is therefore an essential component of every executive's repertoire.

The invitation

When suggesting lunch to a client or colleague, it is usually expedient to state its purpose. This may not only give the guest a reason to decline the offer and save time for both of you, but will also help to avoid circumlocution and edgy table-talk on the day.

He who invites suggests the venue, books the table and pays the bill.

He who accepts should explain in advance any personal dietary restrictions or problems. On the day he should accept the hospitality with grace and without ever alluding to the fact that it is coming out of a corporate budget.

Choosing the restaurant

The host should also ask the guest in advance if he approves of the restaurant. If not, he should have another in mind.

The host should ascertain that the restaurant is not too trendily popular. If it is crammed and noisy it will not be appropriate for a serious business discussion. It is safest to go for a well-established place with a word-of-mouth reputation for quality.

If the guest prefers to leave everything to the host, confirmation should be sought – via his secretary if necessary – about any specific eating regimes or preferences: an aversion to highly spiced foods, a preference for fish or low-calorie food, and so on. The host should then ensure that the restaurant can precisely accommodate the guest's tastes.

Favouritism

Regularly frequenting at least one fine local restaurant is good practice – purely for business purposes, of course – and is just one of the arduous services an executive is obliged to attend to personally. It is advantageous to build personal and company relationships with head waiters and staff. One way of doing so is always to book tables in the name of the organisation as well as the host. Loyal patronisation will be rewarded with individual service and friendly and prestigious acknowledgment. It will also secure tables best suited for confidential conversations, and immunise one from areas subject to excessive kitchen and loo traffic, or the proximity of competitors.

> 'I once asked a leading gastronome which was his favourite restaurant. "The one where I'm known best," he said. Wise words. I'd much rather entertain business guests at an establishment where I'm thoroughly comfortable than at an unfamiliar place with a galaxy of Michelin stars. Making people feel comfortable is one of the keys to successful business entertaining.'
>
> CHRIS KELLY, Writer and broadcaster, and presenter of BBC television's *Food and Drink* programme.

Timing

The host should check the time his guest must leave the restaurant. For his own benefit, it is worth scrutinising his own diary for afternoon commitments. Huge lunches don't leave one with adequate capacity for heavy appointments.

The host should phone his guest the day before the lunch to confirm the time and place; he can supply travel or parking hints if necessary at the same time.

If the host has to cancel, it is clearly best to inform his guest as early as possible and to offer two alternative dates. The guest, if he is the one to cancel, should do likewise.

Hosts should arrive early to check arrangements and to brief the head waiter, cloakroom attendant, barman and others.

When the host is running late, he should phone both the restaurant and his guest's office. If the guest has already arrived at the restaurant, it is the host's duty to ensure he is properly looked after, supplied with refreshment and waited on to the point of genuflection. The magnitude of the host's apologies on arrival should be matched only by the munificence of discreetly distributed tips. The sign of success is that the guest actually enjoys his wait.

If a guest is late, no message has been left, and the host cannot locate him by telephone, forty-five minutes is the optimum waiting time. Unless the guest is from out of town, further lingering is demeaning and may be condoning his guest's lack of consideration. He should make his excuses and depart, leaving a tip for the staff, together with a polite message and contact number should his guest arrive.

Larger parties

When hosting a large party, it is thoughtful to ask guests whom they would like to sit next to. On arrival at the table, guests should remain standing until the host has indicated their seats.

If there is one badly placed seat, facing the kitchen or butted up to the hors-d'oeuvre counter, the host should occupy it to ensure his guests' comfort. Ideally, however, the host should have a position in which he has direct and discreet contact with the serving staff.

At restaurants, people usually prefer to have the best general view possible. Guests in order of priority, and every female, should be offered these prime positions.

Regardless of how many people there are, and of what seniority or sex, the host sits down last. If the host is female and the men refuse to sit until she has done so, it is expedient for her to restrain from playing 'after you's' and submit.

Drinking (see also Chapter 14)

Some people prefer not to drink during the business day (and some companies forbid it), so the host should ensure a plentiful supply of mineral water to slake thirst and minimise the wine order – the quantity, not the quality.

The liquid pressure begins from the moment the chairs scrape under the tables: the cue for the waiter to enquire 'An aperitif?' or even more insidiously 'An appetiser?' The host's tone can set the pattern for moderation or for a drinking spree.

The effects accruing from an over-abundant measure of liquid hospitality include having the guests on their ears before pudding, diminishing the host's ability to control proceedings, and achieving nothing for anyone's business prospects – other than the restaurant owner's.

If alcohol is being served, the host should wait until all the guests' glasses have been filled and then raise his glass to each of them. 'Cheers' is not an appropriate toast in formal company. 'Good health', 'Nice to see you' or 'Thank you for coming' are more appropriate.

Menu selection

The starter and main course are ordered together. The waiter returns after the main course to take orders for pudding ('dessert' is sometimes considered to mean fresh fruit) and coffee.

When there are just two people, it is good practice for the host to consult with his guest and to pass on his order to the waiter. But a host should never order for his guests without consultation. Among the few exceptions is in a speciality restaurant, where the guest has explained his general likes and dislikes and has agreed that the host or the head waiter makes his selection. Guests should be warned of the presence of hot or pungent spices.

If there is to be a particularly large number of people in the party, with strictly limited time, it may be useful to discuss a selection of dishes with them before they arrive and to pre-order so they are served with a minimum of delay.

The host should have budgeted to cover the most expensive items on the menu. The prestige element in entertaining a client is destroyed if he asks his guests to stick to the table d'hôte. The guests, on the other hand, should not order the most expensive items unless encouraged to do so by their host. The host should be courteous in this encouragement, never patronising.

In a business lunch context, such exotic dishes as lobster should be avoided. They can take an inordinate time to prepare and to consume. Furthermore, having to grapple with a crustacean diminishes one's personal effectiveness, as does tangling with strings of pasta and juggling with spare ribs. But see pages 97–9.

Waiting

A guest is not expected to call a waiter to the table; that is the host's exclusive responsibility.

A survey among professional waiters showed that the preferred and most effective way of attracting their attention is to raise the hand, and/or say 'Waiter/Waitress'. Then, if necessary, a slightly louder 'Excuse me'. Clicking fingers and such imperious calls as 'Miss', 'Mate', 'Darling', 'Oy, I say' and the like are rarely appreciated by professionals or anybody else.

Waiters prefer not to be called when involved in serving other tables. Their attention is best captured when moving between tables.

Each time the waiter serves a dish, or offers a side dish, he should be quietly thanked. If you are involved in conversation, you should simply nod or smile. The rule is politely to acknowledge the service as it is delivered. It is not necessary to thank the waiter for placing cutlery or removing empty plates.

Complaining

An adept host will surreptitiously scan his table to ensure that his guests have all they need, as well as to look for signs of dissatisfaction.

A guest should not complain directly to the staff about the food or drink. If the food is badly cooked, or in some way unsatisfactory, he should simply place his knife and fork on his plate, discreetly catch his host's eye and let him deal with it. Without fuss, the host should ascertain the problem and leave the table to tell the waiter. If possible, the situation should be remedied without drama or unduly directing the other guests' attention to it.

If the guests are not receiving adequate attention, a host should not remonstrate with a waiter at the table. It is less embarrassing for him to leave the table and go to the waiter's station, or to the head waiter, to seek a remedy.

Serious complaints for such misdeeds as neglect, poor-quality food or overcharging should be delivered discreetly, and later in writing. It is, again, embarrassing and unpleasant for everyone if the host tries to sort them out vociferously at the table.

Privacy

As the host is entirely responsible for his guest's comfort and welfare, he should restrain from table-hopping or waving to and conversing with a neighbouring party; an inter-table smile at an opportune moment is sufficient. If a client or senior colleague is in the restaurant, the host or guest may excuse himself from the party and briefly go over to pay his respects. It is disrespectful to one's host or guest to conduct business or prolonged conversations with those at other tables.

When someone approaches the table, the host should stand, introduce his guests and not get involved in a long conversation.

Personal points

Handbags and briefcases should not be put on tables, if only for reasons of hygiene.

For the same reason, people should not brush or comb their hair at the table, nor should they chew their fingernails or anything else not on the menu.

Napkins or serviettes

It isn't worth getting involved in the 'napkin or serviette' debate, other than for small talk: either name will do. Some people insist that napkins are cloth and that serviettes are paper. On the other hand, dictionaries talk about paper napkins and cloth serviettes.

Whichever it is, it should be placed on your knees as you sit. After use it should be placed, folded once, on the table. Some people say it should be placed on your chair, but if it is stained and the next passenger is wearing white. . . .

Dabbing the mouth with your napkin is good form; vigorous wiping and checking the debris is not. Mopping perspiration is terrible; blowing the nose unforgivable.

The pay-off

The host should discreetly arrange in advance for the bill to be given to him. Those with supreme savoir-faire spirit themselves from the table at the end of the meal and settle out of sight. Although restaurants are improving, some waiters are still insensitive enough to give the bill to the man, even when the woman is clearly the host. A word in advance will prevent the mistake.

Tipping

In many establishments, a service charge is included in the price or added to the bill. The rate in Britain is at least 10 per cent and at most 15 per cent; any more than that is for service beyond the call of duty.

Be aware of the coercive practice by some restaurant staff of putting the total in the sub-total section of a credit card voucher even though service is included. If that happens, the host should not hesitate to ask whether or not service is included. He should not be intimidated, and should add to the total only if the service has really merited it.

Where a service charge is included or has been added to the bill but service has been seriously lacking, it can be deducted, having privately debated the issue with the head waiter. If the problem was clearly not the table waiter's fault, he can be tipped separately.

As he is not paying the bill, the guest may if he wishes ask the host for his consent to distribute extra staff gratuities.

Who thanks who

The guest thanks the host for his hospitality. The host thanks the guest for attending. They all thank the waiter and head waiter for the meal. Someone, some day, may even thank the chef, although all parading through to the kitchen is a bit over the top. Within two or three days, guests should drop a brief line of further thanks to their host.

Working lunch in the office

Pressure of work often means pushing on through the lunch hour. Where one anticipates doing so with important clients, a buffet should be laid on. Otherwise, in most situations a sandwich lunch is acceptable. Remember to include some sandwiches with non-meat fillings. Accompany them with tea and/or standard and decaffeinated coffee, and perhaps some fresh fruit. Wine may be offered to guests, although many companies nowadays provide just chilled mineral water or juice.

Where possible, an auxiliary member of staff should come in to distribute the plates of sandwiches and the first round of beverages. (After a decent interval he should come back to clear away.) The guests should be served their first sandwich and then asked to help themselves. The food should be offered from the plate and not handled. The plate of sandwiches should be placed nearest to the guests. The home team should not stretch across people to reach for them.

Ideally, everyone should pause from work while eating. An interval for social conversation is useful and refreshing. In addition, conducting business with a mouth full of egg and watercress or splattering globules of food over documents and one another can create a poor and indelible impression.

Sandwiches, particularly thick and mushy ones, are easier to deal with when cut into small, bite-size sections. If not, chewing may be ungainly, fingers messy, clothes stained and guests embarrassed.

Respect for one's guests is exemplified not only by the quality and variety of the food and presentation, but also by the absence of polystyrene, plastic and cardboard. China, stainless steel and linen are more complimentary.

Chapter 13

TABLE MANNERS

JABBING the air with cutlery, chewing while speaking and blowing on the soup are not deadly sins. But when one is entertaining an important client or business contact, such poor table manners can deal a fatal blow to the chances of strengthening the relationship. Even if the client does not actually have to parry the stabs, splashes and general debris, his opinion of his companion will plummet by the mouthful.

But the awkward thing about good table manners is that few people are aware they don't have them until someone tells them so. When that happens, the reactions are, in succession: protest, disbelief, embarrassment, resentment and rejection. This is invariably followed soon afterwards by acceptance. Those in the latter state are ready to acquire a basic knowledge of rudimentary table craft that offers greater poise and self-confidence, not to mention selling capability.

Don't talk, eat – and vice versa

Eating is a quiet and discreet process. We all know that you shouldn't talk with something in your mouth. But what else are business meals for other than to talk?

There are perfectly polite ways of overcoming the problem without compromising good manners. As the basic rule is not to talk with something in your mouth, you need to time when to eat and when to talk. An obvious suggestion is not to start a sentence and then take a bite of food so that everyone is forced to hang on until you have stopped chewing.

Conversation is facilitated by adhering to the general rule that food should be cut (not torn) into small, bite-sized portions.

Perhaps not so obvious is that, when each dish is served, there should be a few seconds of general silence so people can savour their food.

Plates

Side plates for rolls etc. sit on the left. But you can't always play by that rule because not everyone knows it. If there is no side plate, the bread roll should be put on the tablecloth to the left of the setting.

Some plates contain garnish or some other herbage. This is for decoration and not, strictly speaking, for consumption.

Finger bowls, usually with an added slice of lemon or a flower petal, are provided when there is a dish to be eaten with the fingers. They should be used only for the fingertips. Some restaurants also provide a small hand towel; if not, there's the napkin.

Glasses

High-class restaurants may have up to four glasses of various shapes at the top right-hand corner of the place setting.

As a general guide:

- The large one will be for water

- The small-bowled one, with a proportionately long or embellished stem, for white wine

- The medium-sized or large glass for red wine

- The squat or narrow glass for a dessert wine or port.

There may also be a stocky glass known as a copita for sherry, which will be served either as an aperitif or with soup.

If champagne is on order, it will be poured into tall, flute-shaped (sometimes chilled) glasses. Champagne 'saucers' are outdated. They're not suitable for another reason, too – the wideness of the glass means the bubbles escape and the champagne quickly goes flat.

> In many establishments glasses are placed in reverse order to the cutlery – in other words, the nearest glass is the first to use.

The waiter should alleviate any panic or controversy simply by filling the relevant glasses with the appropriate libation and removing any unnecessary ones.

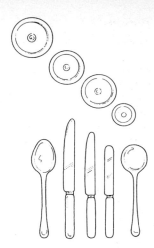

Cutlery

The which-implement-for-which-dish dilemma is easily resolved. The general rule is that you start from the outside and work inwards. If you eat every course, it's fail-safe. Skipping courses should not confuse the issue, as a good waiter will normally remove unnecessary cutlery.

As a general guide to table settings:

- The round soup spoon is normally on the far right of the setting

- On the far left, a small fork for an alternative or additional starter

- Next on the right may be a butter knife, identifiable by the absence of a matching fork on the left

- Then on the right the traditional spatula-like fish knife . . . and, on the left, its fork (fish knives and forks are used less often these days, and a medium-sized knife and fork may be given for the fish course instead)

- Inside the fish knife and fork are the ones for meat; they will normally be the largest

- The dessert spoon and fork will either be inside the meat cutlery, or above the setting. In the upper setting, the fork will be under the spoon with the bowl of the spoon facing to the left and the prongs of the fork to the right.

- All forks and spoons are placed with the hollow up. All knives are placed sharp end facing inwards.

Cutlery control

Forks, spoons, cups, glasses etc. should transport food and drink all the way to the mouth. The body should not bend forward, mouth agape, to meet it halfway.

The knife handle is held inside the palm, thumb below the blade, forefinger straight down the top of the handle. The fork is held similarly, with the forefinger just below the bend. The spoon is held like a pen, but with finger and thumb together, horizontally across the body.

The tips of the knife and fork should remain below the handles. The handles should never rest on the table once the cutlery is in use. When you are chewing, they should be placed vertically on to the respective sides of the plate or held hovering low over it, pointed downwards, with your elbows tucked into your sides.

To signal that you have finished a dish, place the knife/spoon and the fork vertically together on the plate.

When a spoon and fork are laid for pudding, they should both be used. The spoon should be used for cutting and eating. The dessert fork is only for stabilising and pushing the food and it should not go into the mouth.

The art of eating soup

Soup is drunk from the side and not from the end of the soup spoon. The spoon should be dipped sideways into the edge of the bowl nearest you, pushed across and away from you and when just over half full lifted all the way to the mouth. Other than being more elegant than the backward scoop action, the procedure also helps ensure that any drips fall safely back into the bowl. When it is almost empty, the bowl may be tilted away from you and the remains (quietly) scooped up. When you have finished, the spoon is placed back in the bowl.

. . . and dealing with bread

Bread or rolls should not be cut with a knife or bitten whole. They should be broken, a bite-size piece at a time. Butter should be spread on these individual pieces and not on a whole slice or roll.

Managing difficult food

It is best to avoid difficult-to-eat foods at a business meal as the extra attention they require means you'll be giving less attention to your host or guest. You also risk spraying them and yourself with food or embarrassing yourself by not knowing what to do. However there are occasions when you may have no choice – for example at a banquet or dinner where the menu has already been chosen by the host.

Fruit: Bananas – using a knife and fork, cut the two ends off then slice along its length. Fold back the skin, cut off small pieces and eat with the knife and fork.

Grapes – Hold stem in fingers and pluck off the grapes one by one. Spit pips (quietly) into half-clenched hand and put them on the plate.

Peaches, pears, apples, etc. – Hold fruit firmly on plate and quarter with knife. Peel or core with knife and fork. Eat with fingers or, if a very formal occasion, with cutlery. When eating a pudding made with unpitted fruit (e.g. cherries), hold the spoon close to your mouth and quietly and unobtrusively spit the stone into the spoon. Discard on the edge of your plate.

Globe artichokes: Using your hands, pull off the leaves one by one. Dip the broad end into the sauce then, using your teeth, scrape and (quietly) suck off the flesh. If a side-plate has not been provided, stack the debris neatly around the artichoke plate. Remove the remaining thin leaves and inedible furry choke to reveal the lush artichoke bottom. Eat this with knife and fork.

Kebabs: Hold the top of the skewer with your napkin. Slide the fork prongs onto the skewer just below the napkin. Hold the top steady and push the fork down gently and steadily, easing the contents off bit by bit (not in one wild wrench) until they lie in a tidy line on the plate or rice.

Lobster: Best eaten with lobster prongs, nutcrackers and finger bowl. These should be provided by the waiter. The prongs are used for poking into difficult to reach parts of the shell and scooping out the flesh. The nutcrackers are for cracking the claw with. For enthusiasts bent on deep excavation, a bib is appreciated.

Mussels: Use the hands to remove the top shell; bite the mussel off. Alternatively spear the mussels with a fork. Use the shell to scoop up the sauce.

Oysters: Lift the shell to your mouth with your hand, throw back the head, chuck down the contents and soak up the sauce with brown bread. The less hearty may prefer to use the flat side of an oyster fork to prise the flesh from the shell then pierce it with the prongs and swallow it whole, ditto brown bread.

Snails: Use special tongs and a small fork to twist them free of the shell. Use fork to dip them in sauce and convey to mouth.

Spaghetti: Use a fork and spoon. Mix in sauce and cheese with the fork. Hold the fork in the right hand, the spoon in the left. Place the spoon, its bowl facing upwards, under the spaghetti. Push the fork onto the spoon through the spaghetti and twirl onto it a bite-size amount. Eat from the fork.

Vegetables and salads: When served on separate plates, they should be eaten from there. However, if you wish to take advantage of a sauce on your main plate, vegetables can be transferred; they should be cut, a piece at a time, and the sauce patted on with the knife.

Questionable manners

- *When does the eating start?*
  The host should ask his guests to begin as soon as their dish has been served. It makes little sense to allow food to get cold.

- *When is it impolite to talk or lean across someone?*
  Always, because it makes a person feel awkward. If it is unavoidable, an explanation should be offered and an apology made. For the same reason, people should not be leaned across when one is reaching for items on the table. Better always to beg their pardon and ask them to pass the desired object.

- *What happens if eating implements are dropped on the floor?*
  They should be left there and replacements requested.

- *Why are soup bowls tilted backwards and the spoon scooped away from you?*
  A good enough reason is so that hot spillage falls into the plate, not the lap.

- *How does one solve the perennial pea predicament?*
  At less formal occasions, the knife can be abandoned on the side of the plate and the peas scooped on to the upturned fork. Otherwise, a few peas should be speared on the prongs and others pressed lightly on top.

- *How should food be seasoned?*
  Salt should be placed on the side of the plate. The food should then be transported to it and pressed on with the knife. Pepper should be ground or shaken on. Sauces and mustard should be placed on the

plate with a separate spoon. Nothing should be applied until after the food has been tasted.

- *How does one use a toothpick at the table?*
  One does not, if possible. It looks ungainly and unsightly even when performed behind a napkin or with your head twisted away. If something is really troubling you, excuse yourself discreetly and make for the loos.

- *How does one choke politely?*
  If food is caught in the throat and a choking fit is imminent, you should leave quietly and quickly and work it out in the toilet. Unless you are absolutely certain that your last moment is nigh, other people should not have to suffer the coughing and spluttering or be asked to bang your back.

- *How does one remove unwanted food from the mouth?*
  With elegant choreography: by turning your head discreetly away from the table and removing it behind your napkin, leaving it in there, placing it under your chair and asking for another napkin.

- *Should one smoke during the meal?*
  Preferably not. It is bound to upset some people, even if they pretend otherwise. It is also an insult to the chef.

- *When can one smoke after a meal?*
  When everyone at the table and at neighbouring tables has finished eating and no one objects. At very formal functions, not before the national anthem has been played or the MC (master of ceremonies) has made the announcement.

- *And cigars?*
  As above, but they should also be offered around the table.

- *When is the meal formally over?*
  When the host stands.

'There is no such thing as a free lunch in business, but if you do not know the rules of etiquette and acceptable behaviour, it can have the opposite effect on your objective. Then it is expensive, time-wasting and will make you thoroughly uncomfortable.'

REX FLEET, Chairman and Managing Director of NCR UK Ltd.

Chapter 14

WINE MATTERS

YOU need to know a certain amount about wine if you entertain in business. To acquire a decent knowledge, so you can hold your own with the experts, you need to spend a great deal of time browsing through wine books, attending study courses and, of course, imbibing. But really all that is necessary is to be able to select, order and taste wine confidently. One does not need to have 'carbonic maceration' or 'noble rot' on the tip of one's tongue, or to be able to identify the countries of origin of Wormeldange Pietert and Murrumbidgee wines.

For those unfamiliar with the subject, the information in this chapter should keep you safe and confident when dealing with wine lists, wine rituals and most wine waiters.

Choosing wine

Among the sweeping, but safe, wine dictums are:

- red wine with red meats
- white wine with fish and poultry
- rosé, generally as for white
- match the fullness of the wine to the richness of the food.

Better still, ignore all those generalisations and drink what you really like. For example, a light fruity red, a crisp rosé or a dry white go with most foods. There is a risk of embarrassment when pleasing yourself if there is a wine authority in the party. An explanation of why you chose a particular wine should help to uncurl his lip.

For obvious reasons, wine should be selected *after* the party has chosen their food.

101

Before ordering, the host should ask his guests for their wine preferences. If someone requests a genre of battery acid that does not incite universal joy, the host should not show his disapproval; it should be ordered for him – a half-bottle if possible (as this is essentially a business meeting) – and other preferences invited from other guests.

One knows when one has chosen wrongly by the metallic or thin taste when food and wine come into contact, not to mention the metallic expression on any wine expert's face.

If a guest is a known connoisseur, the host may ask him to select the wines. This does not relieve the host of the duty of ensuring that every guest has wine suitable to his meal.

If a knowledgeable guest is not known as a connoisseur, he should restrain from proclaiming his erudition. His best approach is discreetly and modestly to introduce the topic during pre-lunch/dinner drinks, giving his host the option of consulting him or otherwise when the wine list arrives.

In top restaurants a wine waiter or sommelier is usually identified by the cellar key worn around his neck. If one is unfamiliar with his list, it is customary to ask him for his recommendation. This will not normally wipe out your monthly expense account in one swallow; only in exceptional circumstances will a sommelier recommend his most expensive vintage.

'Things have changed dramatically in the last 15 years. People have travelled abroad more and so are generally more knowledgeable about wine. But the etiquette of wine – the ability to choose exactly the correct wine for each dish – is a skill still possessed by the few. It is a skill that commands respect from sommelier and guests alike.'

TONY CARMONA, Head Sommelier at the Savoy Grill, London.

Tasting

All wine should be brought to the host to taste. If it is has been chosen by one of his guests, the host may pass the obligation to him. The host will be shown the bottle to examine the label. The bottle must not be open. If it is, it should be firmly refused.

Having opened the bottle, the sommelier may hand the host the cork. This is to savour the bouquet, as well as to confirm that the cork has not dried out. A dry cork smelling sharply of sherry can mean the wine has become oxidised.

The purpose of tasting wine is not to ascertain whether or not one likes the flavour. (Having ordered it, it should follow that one is familiar with it or that it has been adequately described by the wine waiter.) The reasons for tasting are to check its temperature and condition. Consequently, if more bottles of that same wine are ordered at the same time or afterwards, they should all be tasted by the host. A house wine will not normally be offered for tasting.

Red wine is generally drunk at around room temperature; among the exceptions are some very young reds, which are chilled. White and rosé should be chilled and placed in a wine cooler during the meal.

A good red wine should be opened and brought to room temperature ('chambré') at least half an hour before drinking, so the host should order it on arrival at the restaurant. He should explain to his guests that this does not over-ride any alternative wines they may wish to order. Ordering a fine wine is a compliment to the guests, so they should gracefully consider trying at least a taste.

Rejecting

A defiled wine is not difficult to detect. Other than the sensation that one has just sipped from a Victorian swimming pool, the other characteristics are:

- a vinegary taste that burns the throat

- a brown tinge in a white wine, or a deep brown colour in a red

- a musty, mouldy or decaying taste, with no redeeming aroma

- cloudiness.

Still white wine that is cloudy is clearly off, probably through an undesirable secondary fermentation. The same goes for sparkling white wine. Cloudy red wine can mean something is wrong. On the other hand it could be that the sediment has not been allowed to settle at the bottom of the bottle.

When the cork is moist from top to bottom, completely dried out or distorted, the wine is probably impaired – or 'corked'.

If the taster suspects – but is not certain – that the wine is bad, he should discreetly ask the wine waiter to taste it. A sommelier may have a tasting spoon for that purpose. Should this fail to resolve the matter, the host should politely request another bottle. A sommelier's tantrum is far less of a peril than that of poisoning one's clients or even one's colleagues.

Rejecting your wine will normally cost the restaurateur nothing. His supplier will normally replace it for him free of charge.

Serving wine

Having tasted a sample of the wine, the host should ask the waiter to serve it to his guests. The waiter should pour it gently, treating it with respect and not disturbing any sediment. Glasses should not be filled more than two-thirds – the top third is where the bouquet lives. After the guests have been served, the waiter returns to charge the host's glass.

Although the wine waiter should ensure that no glass stays empty, it is the host's ultimate responsibility. So if the waiter is otherwise engaged, the host may pour. The glass remains on the table and the bottle is brought to it, even if it means the host circumnavigating the table.

If a guest does not wish to have his glass refilled, he should simply say so. Only when he is in the middle of a conversation should he cover the top of his glass with his hand.

Champagne

Proper champagne comes from the strictly defined Champagne region in France, and is the result of secondary fermentation in the bottle.

If that process takes place anywhere outside the region, the bottles may look similar but the labels will say '*méthode champenoise*' (or less exotically 'naturally fermented in the bottle'). They may have less prestige, not to mention a considerably smaller price tag, but some experts maintain they can taste just as good. If it still looks like champagne, but the secondary fermentation occurs out of the bottle, the label will say '*cuve close*' – which isn't bad either. It is safe to offer these, in rapidly descending levels of prestige, to guests.

Inside most other champagne-style bottles will be simply the cheaper carbonated or 'foot-pump' wine.

Opening champagne

If the host wishes to open the bottle himself, he should not try the flamboyant '*méthode Grand Prix*' which is done for show, to soak the assembly and to knock out the teeth of the runners-up. The cork is seriously dangerous in flight, so the bottle should always be aimed away from the table and in a safe direction.

The palm of the hand should be placed over the cork as the wire cage is unfastened. The *bottle* itself should be slowly rotated, holding on to the cork and the cage. It should be steered into a 45 degree angle, and the cork gently twisted off and held, resulting in the minimum of wasted foam and a well-bred 'pop'.

Bin ends

Beware of being a vintage bore; there is a limit to how much information about wine that people can, or wish to, soak up. And remember the old Latin tag '*In vino veritas*', which translated into neo-business language means 'Don't over-indulge or you'll give too much away.'

Pretentiousness is dangerous. If in doubt about wine or wine lore don't guess, ask an expert.

Chapter 15

RECEPTION HOSTING AND GUESTING

RECEPTIONS, buffets and cocktail parties are integral to many companies' marketing strategies and large investments are made in the venues, catering and presentation at business hospitality events. The social graces required for them are, therefore, important to all executives. Becoming accomplished in them is an agreeable way of expanding your business perspective and capability.

The art of business hospitality can be divided arbitrarily into three main arenas:

- The reception, which can be for a press and/or trade announcement and can include special guests of honour or speakers

- The buffet, celebrating a specific event or person

- The cocktail party, including annual/regular celebrations.

The basic ground rules of etiquette are similar for each of them – with the invitation itself indicating the level of formality.

The location

Hotels usually have the expertise, along with the necessary logistical facilities, for business parties. Next come good restaurants.

If the office environment is pleasant it is acceptable to hold social gatherings there, but it can disrupt working routines. It could also mean that on the morning after, the staff would face the smell of stale alcohol, overflowing ashtrays and discarded glasses or guests behind the filing cabinet.

Offices are not the best places for press receptions, particularly if classified company documents are stored there. If the party combines a social with a business purpose, it can be held at the senior executive's home. With spouses and partners in attendance the occasion will be more enjoyable, but it is less appropriate for long, formal presentations.

Live music – for example a string quartet, a dance band or a pianist – is usually a good idea at occasions where guests are invited to bring partners. But it is expedient to ensure they are experienced at such occasions. Apart from having an appropriate repertoire, they will need to know how to pitch the volume low enough so people do not have to shout at one another, but not so low as to be irritating.

The invitation

Invitations should be as comprehensive as possible so guests do not need to phone to enquire about dress, duration and so on. The following minimum information should be included:

- from whom
- to whom
- type of occasion
- date
- times
- venue
- dress
- RSVP and address.

For example:

> Sir Bryce Fowler, KBE, Chairman of Fowler International Ltd, has pleasure in inviting
>
> *Mr and Mrs Peter Guest*
>
> to a Cocktail Party to celebrate the publication of *The Fowler Story* at Fleming House, 33 Wharf Road, Brighton, BN1 2N
>
> 4 to 6pm on Tuesday, 4 July 1993
>
> RSVP Ms Elizabeth Bush, at Fowler House and on 0273–9382

Replies to such invitations should be prompt, whether affirmative or not. An acceptance can take the following form:

107

Dear Ms Bush,

Thank you for the invitation from Sir Bryce Fleming to attend the cocktail party to celebrate the publication of *The Fleming Story*. My wife, Lorna, and I are very happy to accept.

Yours sincerely,

Peter Guest

Refusals should contain the reason why:

Dear Ms Bush,

Thank you very much for the invitation from Sir Bryce Fowler to attend the cocktail party celebrating the publication of *The Fowler Story*. Unfortunately I will be out of town on that day, and so with regret am unable to attend. My wife and I hope the occasion – and the book – will both be a great success.

Yours sincerely,

Peter Guest

A formal 'third person' reply may be used to invitations from people with whom one does not have a personal acquaintance. For example:

Dear Madam,

Peter Guest would like to thank you for your invitation to the cocktail party celebrating the publication of *The Fowler Story*. [EITHER:] He is pleased to accept and looks forward to meeting Sir Bryce and Lady Fowler on July 3rd. [OR:] He regrets that due to a prior arrangement, he will be unable to attend.

Yours faithfully,

Horace Henry
Personal Assistant to Mr Peter Guest.

Ensuring a good acceptance rate
There are two cardinal rules in ensuring that the right people attend your business function in the right numbers:

- First, before deciding on a date and time, check that they do not clash with other 'trade' occasions
- Second, invitations should be sent out well in advance:
  - Four to six weeks ahead of a luncheon, cocktail, breakfast or tea party or late afternoon reception
  - Four months for an important dinner function with out-of-town guests
  - Six to eight months for a national or international conference.

Other than for really unique and irresistible occasions, invitations should always be sent to more guests than you anticipate turning up – too few is invariably worse than too many.

Reply cards

Where necessary, a reply card should be enclosed (together with a stamped addressed envelope), printed with at least the following details:

Mr and Mrs Response of RP Ltd
are able/are unable to attend
your reception on February 29th.

If a guest is unable to attend, he should consider sending a brief explanatory note. This should be more detailed than playwright George Bernard Shaw's response to a famous society hostess of the twenties who sent this invitation:

Mrs . . . . .
At home on
Saturday 14 March

His reply was: 'GBS ditto'.

Monitoring replies

Someone should be made responsible for the guest list and for monitoring replies. Where responses are slow in coming, phone calls can be made to secretaries – or direct, if the relationships are personal – to establish people's intentions.

Cancellation

If an occasion has to be cancelled or postponed, all guests must be informed in writing, with follow-up phone calls to confirm they have received the notice.

Human cocktails

Successful parties depend on an interesting mix of guests, but the list should be combed for explosive combinations. Inviting deadly rivals, business or otherwise, may induce an embarrassing maelstrom into which the host will be sucked.

Dress (see also Chapter 19)

At all social business gatherings other than strictly formal ones a man should wear a lounge suit, shirt and tie. In more informal companies, for example those in creative or media fields, dress is more relaxed, although it is always worth considering wearing a jacket.

A woman should wear a dress of a more feminine variety than her normal business outfit. Alternatively a smart suit with tailored skirt or well-cut trousers. Heels may look more elegant but flat shoes or ones with low heels are preferable as she may be standing a lot. A hat will probably be over the top.

If possible, reception outfits should be brought to work and changed into so they look crisp for the occasion. When there is no time for a complete switch of wardrobe between the office and the reception, you should change something. A man can change his shirt and tie, or at least his tie. A woman can change her blouse, don a smart jacket, add a silk scarf or a piece of dressy jewellery. The aim is to look perceptibly smarter, without appearing overdressed.

Timing

Two hours is the optimum duration for most business parties. Times of arrival and departure should be printed clearly on the invitation, adding 'sharp' to the times if necessary. Guests should have up to thirty minutes' grace, specified on the invitation in the form: '5.30pm for 6pm'. The first half-hour enables them to mingle, warm up and settle down before the formalities begin.

Although lunchtime invitations help ensure a good turn-out, the drawback is that company staff may not end up in perfect condition for a full afternoon's work.

The optimum time to start most kinds of business parties is half an hour after the customary end of the business day, e.g. 5.30pm in some sectors, 7pm in others; 8.30pm is too late unless it is for dinner.

When to arrive? Five to ten minutes after the specified start time will probably feel most comfortable. Arriving before the stated time may not be appreciated, as preparations may be continuing until the last minute.

Press receptions

Where a press announcement is to be made, receptions should start no later than 5.30pm, for deadline reasons. Friday evenings should be avoided, as there may be a lack of available journalists. Saturdays are not good either, as most feature pages have already gone to press and there is a limit to the space available for non-essential news stories.

The time that a speech or announcement is to be made should be printed on the invitation or press release. It should be early in the proceedings – before people become too involved in fifth estate activities.

News should normally be announced before handing out a press release. If not, the audience will be thumbing through it and reaching their own conclusions before you have had a chance to state yours. Every company representative should be briefed with a single, unambiguous story. If it is a hot potato, junior employees should refer press enquiries to senior or PR executives. And company representatives should refrain from drinking.

If the story is of a product release that will elicit wide yet benign interest, ensure that there are sufficient home-team employees to distribute hand-outs and care individually for journalists.

At a press reception, nothing is off the record. Don't risk discussing confidential background information – it puts the journalist in an invidious position and he may have to publish and damn the friendship. The dimensions of hospitality are often in inverse relation to the amount of coverage received. After all, if you have a story of real news value, why all the trappings? Tea and biscuits would do. Journalists attend press receptions as a matter of daily business routine, so the host should not expect thank you letters. Should he get reasonable coverage, *he* should be the one to send them.

Unless the reception is for genuinely newsworthy reasons, you cannot blame journalists for coming along for purely free-loading purposes.

Food

Business parties can accommodate from a dozen to 100 people, so food is a major item. Nuts are not enough. In the evening supper need not be provided, but attractive food is important as it will prevent guests from drinking on empty stomachs. Canapés, small sandwiches and other finger foods are favoured. If hot dishes are supplied, they should be tasty rather than filling – such as small quiches and scampi.

> Tables and chairs should be craftily arranged, so as not to convey a 'sit-down meal' feeling which discourages guests from circulating.

Drink

Champagne is the mark of the importance of the occasion. Otherwise at cocktail parties drinks can be a combination of wines, spirits and even cocktails!

Mineral water is *de rigueur* nowadays. Other non-alcoholic drinks, such as juices and cordials, should also be available.

> It is worth taking as much trouble over the selection of soft drinks as over the alcohol.

Greetings

At the start of a formal occasion, appropriate company representatives may stand in a short receiving line by the entrance, with the main host first in line. On a strictly business occasion, the host's spouse will not be in the receiving line. The members of the receiving line should not hold drinks or cigarettes.

The line is not the place for long conversations. But it is useful for those unaccustomed to small talk to arm themselves with a standard ice-breaking topic. Even the weather or road conditions will do, starting with the old conversational one-two 'Have you come far?' followed with 'What was the traffic/weather like?'

> Tone and warmth are more important than content when making people feel welcome.

If a master of ceremonies has been engaged, he will announce the guests' names as they arrive. He will check the numbers of those waiting to be introduced and, if their number becomes uncomfortably large, he will inform the line so they can condense their conversations.

Names

Guests are often uneasy as they enter. Incorporating their names in a friendly greeting helps relax them, as in 'John Hail, this is Martin Vista.' 'How do you do Mr Vista, nice to meet you' . . . that also helps you memorise it.

Memory works by association. Most memory schools recommend associating a name with a distinctive picture. For example, as you are introduced to Mr Masters, picture him wearing a mortar board. The technique does work, with practice.

If you forget a name you can admit it, which is forgivable if you have just met someone. Alternatively, you could lie through your teeth as in, 'I'm sorry, I've forgotten your name . . .'

'John.'

'No, I remember John. It's your surname that has escaped me.' (Or vice versa.)

Another gambit, though requiring some dexterity, is to suggest that people introduce themselves while you pop off to get them all a drink. Asking people for the spelling of their names is a useful technique. Even when you are countered with 'S-m-i-t-h', you can always say 'I wondered if it was with a 'y'.

It is worth arming yourself with these old tricks in the knowledge that the tension of a formal business occasion can addle the mind. A case famous in the car marketing industry concerns a sales manager faced with a terribly important fleet buyer. The salesman's mind went blank and he couldn't remember his own wife's name (after ten years of marriage). He said 'This is, er . . . em, my wife.' She added 'Susan.' He will never be allowed to forget that.

Hosts' duties

Representatives of the host company should be assigned certain duties. Essentially, their mission is to ensure the success of the occasion, both socially and commercially. So, for example, the safety catches should be off pocket books to allow for speedy access to business cards; and pen and paper should be accessible for writing down addresses and contact names.

As hosts, company representatives should be made responsible for introducing guests who may be of interest to one another, and for separating guests who are not. To ensure that no guest is left isolated or neglected, they should introduce him into a group and stay long enough to ensure he is assimilated.

A host should ensure that guests have all they require and are being properly supplied with food and drink. If no waiter is available, the host should fetch and carry. This does not make him a waiter, just a good host.

Conversation

There are countless conversational gambits, many of which may feel unnatural but are worth employing if only to help a guest unwind and feel wanted. 'How do you know the host?' is an easy approach.

Otherwise, nobody has ever devised a better, more stimulating technique than getting a guest to talk about himself. Politely asking people what they do is a simple, fail-safe ploy to which people invariably respond positively, except perhaps when the reply is 'I'm your boss.'

> 'Certain topics of conversation are best avoided in business, particularly at lunches for large numbers. Racist or feminist remarks are clearly uncalled for and are likely to be offensive. Politics and religion are also minefields for the unwary.'
>
> ALAN J. FROST, Managing Director of Abbey Life.

The party's over

The drinks should unobtrusively begin to dry up about fifteen minutes before the end. Waiters and bartenders should begin slowing down and then withdraw their services altogether at the allotted time.

A smooth way of clearing a room is to arrange to have a 'leaving gift' – perhaps chocolates, a customised pen or calculator – which should be distributed near to finishing time. This can be prefaced by a short speech of thanks to the guests for their attendance. The gifts should also be available at the exit immediately after the formalities, for those who cannot stay till the very end.

Guests are expected to observe the stated time for departure, particularly as the organisers will have carefully scheduled their clearing away procedures, staff times and so on. Staying late to finish conversations and bottles in such circumstances will not please or flatter those responsible. At the departure time, serious discussion groups should break off and re-muster elsewhere.

Chapter 16

ENTERTAINING TABOOS

HOWEVER much time, money and trouble is invested in business hospitality events, they can all be nullified if the host company's staff do not know how to conduct themselves properly. Bad behaviour on such occasions can, at a stroke, downgrade business relationships and harm the prestige of the whole company.

Such behaviour is rarely deliberate – it is more likely to be caused by a lack of awareness, or even nerves. This chapter flags some of the common hazards encountered at business hospitality events, suggests ways of avoiding them, and, if prevention isn't possible, proposes certain remedies.

Negative behaviour

The business cocktail party is designed primarily for cultivating contacts, not for closing contracts. A company representative should not not use a party to sell if it has been announced as a social occasion. At most he should ask a guest for a card or address, and do his selling at a later date.

Dispensing brochures is an imposition on guests. If desperate, literature should be left at the reception piont to be collected as the guest is leaving.

Company people should never stand around in corporate bodies of more than three. It is unfriendly and intimidating.

Representatives of the host company must not under any conditions make disparaging remarks about the occasion. If they are bored, this may be very hard to resist. But it will serve only to spoil the enjoyment of people who may actually be having a good time. Furthermore, criticism has wings and a random flight plan, so it is bound to sail straight into the wrong ears.

The body as enemy

A dash of humour stirred in relieves all the following embarrassing situations very much more effectively than remaining poe-faced and intense about it all. The exceptions are 'Breaking wind' and 'Rumbling tummy' (see page 118).

Sneezing and coughing

These are not supposed to be shared experiences; the cultivated expectorator turns or walks away from everyone and covers his mouth.

Hiccups

Incessant hiccups quickly become a general irritant. The sufferer is best advised to withdraw until the spasm – often caused by tension – is over. Drinking water from the wrong side of a glass is said to help some.

Bad breath

The cure for bad breath is more complicated. First, because it is not the afflicted who suffer most. And second, a person with bad breath may be the last to know. He may think that people who flinch when he speaks simply have a nervous tic. Even when people flatten themselves against walls as he passes, the penny may still not drop. A peer or senior must tell the poor sufferer and recommend short-term remedies.

If we can say yes to any of the following questions, we ourselves could be offenders:

- Is our tummy upset, rumbly or acidy?
- Did we consume garlic, onions, alcohol or heavily spiced food in the last twelve hours?
- Do we smoke? Are we suffering from acute ill health or serious stress?
- Do we have any bad teeth?
- Do we avoid dental check-ups?

Short-term remedies include deodorising mouth sprays or capsules. If they are not immediately available, sucking mints, tea leaves or parsley helps a little. Long-term answers are a course of dental hygiene bolstered by specific mouthwashes prescribed by a dentist, dental surgery, or a review of your diet.

Even those whose insides are normally like mountain streams should be careful not to stand too close to people at drinking parties. As with smoking, drinking adds an unappealing potency to the breath at close quarters.

117

Yawning

If a yawn overcomes you, the action sequence is to turn away, cover the mouth and find an excuse that won't make your companion think you are bored with him. If you have been so busy you have not been getting enough sleep, that is a reasonable excuse. Another is that your drink is succeeding in unwinding you.

Breaking wind

The offender should avoid laughter wherever possible. If the occurrence can be ignored, it should be. Otherwise, the offender should apologise briefly and carry on with his conversation, which gives people something else to concentrate on and helps prevent embarrassment, offence or hysterics.

Rumbling tummy

As breaking wind above, perhaps mixed with a short comment about an impending mealtime.

Spilling food and drink

These should not be the overture to a prolonged chorus of apologies and faffing around but should be dealt with quickly and with as little table disruption as possible. You should apologise and dispose of large pieces of debris if necessary, but without falling to your knees to gather tiny fragments, be they glass, blancmange or anything. The host should be told, or better still the catering staff who have the appropriate tools to carry out the job. You should apologise to them, and leave them to it.

> 'I once presided at a business banquet at a top hotel where a fight broke out and at other occasions where bread rolls have filled the air. I'm not saying that these are common occurrences, but bad behaviour of any kind defeats the whole purpose of the affair. This is a great pity; the British ability to run a really first-class banquet or reception is the envy of the world, and an unrivalled business asset.'
>
> MARTIN NICHOLLS, General Secretary of the National Association of Toastmasters.

Controlling bores

Bores come in two main categories: he who talks because he is nervous
. . . and he who has never learned to listen. The former should be cultivated, until he feels more confident, and then introduced into a warm
circle. The following observations apply to the latter, more brazen,
type.

Going to the toilet is the knee-jerk reaction to avoiding bores. Unfortunately if the offender is of the same sex he may declare 'That's the best
idea since sliced bread' and accompany you.

- Safer is to locate someone you have to speak to urgently

- More subtle is to apologise for monopolising him and suggest you
  should both circulate more

- Unwise is to introduce him to someone else, because that someone
  could turn out to be an important business contact for you who will
  remember the gesture

- Perilous is to look bothered and complain that the smoke or lack of air
  is getting to you and you need fresh air; he may suddenly feel the
  same way.

Submitting is often the only recourse, particularly if the bore is an
important client or someone senior to you in the company. In which
case, one can try to cling to consciousness by constantly changing the
subject. It works with most bores, because so long as they hear the
sound of their own voice they don't worry too much what it is saying. So
don't ever be nervous of interrupting them at reasonable intervals,
particularly when you preface your verbal lunges with variations on the
theme of 'I'd be interested to hear your opinion on . . .'. The trick is
being able to remember what they've already covered.

Dealing with drunks

A drunk is an embarrassment and a threat. An embarrassment to everyone and a threat to the investment made in the occasion, particularly if
he represents the host company.

Those observations are obvious; fortunately so are the signs to watch
out for in the susceptible. The portents of gathering inebriation, for
those who can't believe it is happening in front of them, include:

- a slightly raised voice

- speech speeding up

- deepening or blotchy complexion
- physical agitation
- belligerent tone.

At the first signs of any of the above, summon a colleague and guide the victim out of the room and to a location where, with someone at his side, he can begin to sober up.

These relatively benign symptoms can usually be dealt with without fuss. This will not be the case when they have progressed into the classic unfocused eyes, swaying frame and propensity for body contact. A lush who has got out of control before you can reach him may be surrounded by guests pretending not to notice, but who are actually too embarrassed to deal with him. The mission of the host company representatives is to get him out of there.

The key to handling a drunk is to resist treating him like a silly child or a damned nuisance. Instead you must maintain your respect for him in everything you do and say. The inebriated are frequently very sensitive to tone and atmosphere, so be careful not to patronise or bully. By maintaining a firm and polite demeanour you have the best chance of cooperation.

Summon whatever assistance is available, preferably a waiter – if not, a colleague of yours or the drunk's – and escort the inebriate from the room. Having settled him in a quiet room with some water and coffee, allow him to recover his equilibrium. Then get him out of the place. Even if he claims to be fully recovered his reappearance will disconcert other guests, and there will be continual anxiety that he'll plunge back into his earlier state. Call a cab or arrange some other transport and have someone take him straight home.

Chapter 17

Events Cultural, Sporting and Rewarding

NO longer is entry to royal events, first-nights and major sports occasions the exclusive preserve of the privileged and the celebrated. Corporate person has bought in to most of them. Entertaining at this level is an enjoyable means of pleasing clients and impressing them with one's social clout.

The business world bids high for the most desirable seats and vantage points. It is increasingly penetrating the inner social circle as sponsors of events and cultural enterprises across the sporting and artistic calendar. (For full information on the latter, contact the Confederation of British Industry's Association for the Business Sponsorship of the Arts – see Useful Addresses.)

But it is not enough simply to arm oneself with one's priceless tickets, don one's formal attire and steer one's taffeta-clad partner past deferential commissionaires. You need to know what to do when you get through the gate.

The royal garden party

This is one occasion you can't officially buy entry to, and attendance is by invitation only. You must be part of an organisation that comes to the attention of a sponsor – the Lord Lieutenant of your county for example. Invitations are sent on behalf of the Queen by the Lord Chamberlain (phone Buckingham Palace for details).

You do not have to reply to confirm your attendance. Royal invitations are in the nature of commands, so if you cannot make it you must have a very good reason or you could be struck off future guest lists.

All you need to know to graze the imperial pastures at the rear of Buckingham Palace is contained on the detailed invitation. This includes where to park and, as with all official royal occasions, it forbids cameras without special authorisation.

Umbrellas are not allowed either, so it will probably rain. Dress accordingly – in something that won't make you look like a drowned moth after the downpour. Ladies wear formal but pretty afternoon dresses – trousers are frowned upon – and hats. Men dress formally, in morning suits (which can be hired) lounge suits or uniform, but no chains of office.

The gates open at 3.15pm. If you arrive an hour early, the queue will already be about a quarter of a mile long, so be prepared for a long, slow shuffle.

The royal family appear at 4pm. They walk through the gardens along an avenue of guests, occasionally stopping and chatting. If special presentations are to be held, they make their way to the appropriate area.

You will not suddenly be plucked from the crowd to be presented. You will have been forewarned. A member of the royal household will have made contact in advance and gleaned a few details about yourself, including whether or not you have met any of the royals before. You will be told where to be, when to be there and what to do when you arrive.

It is all tightly organised, leaving virtually nothing to chance. The only responsibility you have is to maintain the connection between your brain and mouth when you are spoken to. The Queen and Queen Mother are addressed as 'Your Majesty', subsequently 'Ma'am' (pronounced 'Mam') and the Duke of Edinburgh, 'Your Royal Highness', then 'Sir'. All other members of the royal family are addressed initially as 'Your Royal Highness,' subsequently as 'Sir' or 'Ma'am'.

Nerves should not be too great an issue when your majestic millisecond arrives, as the royal family are accustomed to making allowances for the sudden catatonic condition of their guests. The simple rule when presented to royalty is not to speak first – that is their prerogative. If they do engage you in conversation it will probably be about your job or the event you are attending, so it's worth rehearsing a short statement. Do not be disappointed if they break off quickly, as their movements are usually timed to the second.

Men should bow their heads when meeting the Queen. Women should drop a brief curtsey: slightly bent knees, never a full body collapse.

If there is time after the presentations, the royals may do some general mingling before going off to their own tent for tea at 5pm. Guests are shown into other tea tents around the garden.

A royal garden party is normally a very formal occasion, requiring strict etiquette. But that doesn't mean you should be intimidated by the stature of you fellow guests. All kinds of people are invited, most of whom will not be gentry. This may be a once-in-a-lifetime opportunity to meet some exceptionally interesting and worthy people (as well as some very uptight ones), so you should take full advantage and mix.

Dead on 6pm the drums will roll, spines will stiffen and the national anthem will be played. The royals will then depart, leaving you to start your shuffle towards the exit. It is permissible to leave early, but your departure should be arranged through a member of staff.

Royal Ascot

Since it was established in 1711 by Queen Anne, Royal Ascot has been a leading event of the London 'season'. It is the only racecourse in the country still owned by the Crown, and the only sporting event at which the Queen herself and members of her family attend on a daily basis. Their carriage procession through the Golden Gate and along the straight mile signals the start of each day's racing.

Much business entertaining goes on, often organised by corporate hospitality firms who provide champagne receptions, morning coffee and afternoon tea, luncheons with all the trimmings, car park passes and entry tickets to the Grandstand, Paddock and Tattersall's.

Tickets are issued by the Ascot Office at St James's Palace (see Useful Addresses). Applications begin in January. Further information on ticket procedures is published the previous month in the court pages of the *Times* and *Daily Telegraph*.

The Royal Enclosure

Strict rules are applied from the start. When applying for Royal Enclosure tickets you must state how many people you wish to bring. You will be sent a 'Sponsor Form', which you must have signed either by someone who knows the Queen or who has attended at least four times before. Even if you can fulfil those conditions, your application will not guarantee tickets. Admission is entirely at the discretion of Her Majesty's representative. He may bar people of bad reputation, bankrupts, those with criminal records, and so on.

Dress in the Royal Enclosure is formal. Those improperly dressed will simply not be admitted. Men wear morning suits and top hats, women formal day dresses. Hats are obligatory for women; publicity seekers wear the freakish kind.

Cameras are prohibited. Members of the royal family must not be pointed at, stared at or approached, particularly not for racing tips!

THE COMPLETE BOOK OF BUSINESS ETIQUETTE

There is a bar at which very expensive champagne is *de rigueur*. Behaviour is expected to be discreet. Being in the Royal Enclosure at Ascot means not screaming loudly when your horse is winning and certainly not when it's losing.

Horse racing (general)

The Jockey Club is the governing body of flat racing, the season for which runs from the end of March to the middle of November. National Hunt or 'steeplechasing', governed by the National Hunt Committee, is from August to the following Whitsun and includes the Grand National at Aintree. Other important courses are at Epsom, Newmarket, Goodwood, Doncaster, Sandown Park, York and Ascot.

The three most important enclosures are: the Club or Members', Tattersall's and the Silver Ring. Tickets are required for the first two. If you cannot get into an enclosure you will not impress the client. Men should wear suits, and women smart afternoon dresses and hats if possible. In winter, tweeds are in.

Many businesses hire marquees for their guests and provide a champagne buffet or picnic. Watching the horses is optional. Some companies sponsor races and prizes or run concurrent charity drives. Otherwise, it is plainly inadvisable to be seen placing large bets by clients and employees.

Henley

Established over a century and a half ago, and held at the height of summer, Henley Regatta is one of the most colourful sporting/social events of the year. Henley the town, nestles prettily at the foot of the Chilterns, with wide river views. It's necessary to arrive very early to avoid having to navigate through its legendary thick traffic. To make a bigger impression, it is a splendid idea to book into one of the town's lovely old hotels for the previous night.

The enclosures

The most splendidly English sights are to be had from and in the Stewards' Enclosure, but entrance to that is by invitation only. One social step down is the Regatta Enclosure. You pay at the gate to get in and to while away a pleasant enough afternoon.

Dress in the enclosures may seem casual, but it is strictly regulated. The chaps wear summer suits, blazers or sports jackets with ties or cravats, straw boaters, and college or club accessories. The ladies wear pretty dresses or below-the-knee skirts – not trousers.

Behaviour is English. Restrained. One does not shout. Light braying and quacking is acceptable so long as it does not go above the prevailing decibel level. Not a lot of cheering goes on. Refined applause is more the mark – and not much of that either, as it is the minority who go for the actual racing.

> Getting legless and starting to sing rugger songs is the cue for a selection of the forty elected stewards at Henley to eject the offender before the second verse.

Costly buffet lunch and drinks are served in a marquee – and people try not to get caught drinking anything other than champers or Pimms. Picnicking outside the enclosure is permitted and has become something of a tradition.

It is advisable to leave late. A fair plan is to dine languorously at one of the restaurants in the area before motoring back through thinning traffic.

Cowes

On the northern tip of the Isle of Wight, Cowes can be reached easily by car or passenger ferry. Once there, lunching, dining and posing on the deck of a sponsored or chartered yacht is the way many corporate entertainers and entertainees enjoy this classic regatta week.

Ten thousand or so sailors thrash up and down the Solent during Cowes Week, usually launched at the beginning of August. In their wake, thousands of sightseers arrive for the sails, surging in and out like the morning and evening tides and bobbing around the quays, restaurants and clubs that lie around the event's administrative hub, the Island Sailing Club.

You can regard the Cowes schedule in one of two ways: either the sport starts at 9.30am, followed by the socialising at nightly yacht club balls and champagne binges . . . or everything starts in the evenings and ends in the early hours in time for the participants to change out of their dinner jackets or party dresses and into their pumps and lifejackets, and fall into their vessels. Either way, it's a stimulating and exhausting experience, but with a rigid and restricted social structure from the royal yacht *Britannia* downwards – but not very far downwards.

125

Everything centres on a handful of yacht clubs. Entry to their premises and to parties on their vessels are by invitation only. Temporary membership to most of them will smooth the social passage. This may be obtained by applying to their secretaries. Royal Yacht Squadron membership however, is obtainable only through the introduction of a member. The RYS is extremely formal: women wear dresses and occasionally hats and most of the men sport a collar and black or navy tie, yachting suit or reefer jacket, and white or grey flannels. (Invitations will state what form of dress is required.) The same garb is worn in the other clubs, although women do not often wear hats and can wear smart trousers.

For most social occasions aboard large yachts, men wear collars and ties and women wear day-length dresses, full skirts or tailored trousers.

Lord's Cricket Ground

The home of the Marylebone Cricket Club (MCC) and of the regulating body of English cricket is also one of the great sexist bastions, so if you are thinking of somewhere to take mixed business company, skip this section. Should you be in the Members' Pavilion when play is about to begin, the ladies will be politely but resolutely shoo'd into the public area as they are prohibited there during play.

Unless otherwise advised, men must wear jacket, collar and tie in the Pavilion. Cameras should not be in evidence.

For men who enjoy one another's company, the Pavilion is a jolly relaxing place to spend the day. A smattering of clapping, a hum of comment and the occasional yelp of quickly rebottled excitement is about as resonant as it gets. Shouting is seriously frowned upon and could get the offender chucked out.

Prolonged booing or jeering are always bad form and very bad manners at any sporting event.

The public areas are quite self-controlled too, except when England is playing the West Indies, at which time there is a constant happy cacophony. The Ashes matches against Australia are renowned for the 'wit' and language of the expatriates in the crowd. You can wear more or less what you like in the public areas, but white shirt, grey flannels and blazer make a contribution to the traditional ambience.

Despite its odd customs, this is still the great cricket club, and demand for tickets, especially for Test matches, is always high.

Members apply for them in January; they become available to the public in March.

Wimbledon

The All England Club at Wimbledon circulates booking details of their summer Open Tournament in December of each year. Obtaining tickets can be pot luck, so unless you are a member, or yours is a sponsoring company, you may be unable to make it a regular corporate outing.

The Members' Enclosure is an elegant location where jackets and ties and generally smart dress are obligatory and where conversation is muted so as not to distract the players slogging it out at close hand. The most prestigious Wimbledon tickets are for the Centre Court on the men's or women's final day, but the men's semi-finals day is sometimes the more exhilarating.

If you and your guests intend eating at Wimbledon and indulging in the traditional strawberries and cream, take a large cash float.

Opera and ballet

These are occasions for truly elegant and certainly expensive business entertaining. The cream of English opera is performed at the Royal Opera House, as is some of the best ballet. You need to book months ahead for the most prestigious performances and artists.

To enjoy them in real style, a box (or 'ashtray' as they are called backstage) should be reserved. Booking seats elsewhere may submit your business guests to the scrum that takes place in the 'crush bars' during the intervals. How much more agreeable to close the door on the less prodigal and order a platter of smoked salmon sandwiches and a bottle of champagne from your own waiter. Sometimes it's possible to eat, literally, at intervals through the performance. Starters are consumed before the overture, and the following courses served in your box or the restaurant after each act. Advance booking is essential for this.

At most ballet and opera gala nights at the ROH, as well as at other theatres, black tie and evening dresses are worn (see Chapter 19 for details). At other times, suits and smart dresses are appropriate.

Late-coming is dealt with ruthlessly after curtain-up. The tardy may be made to wait until a suitable pause in the performance – which can be the end of the first Act!

Arriving early is certainly a good idea, as it enables you to book refreshments for the interval – if the house offers such a facility. More important for the uninitiated, it gives you time to read the programme notes so you know what is happening on stage – thereby enhancing your enjoyment and prestige.

Applause can be tricky. Dedicated opera lovers and balletomanes try to restrain themselves from clapping before the dying notes of a piece. But how do you know when the end is nigh? You don't, unless you have seen it before. So newcomers should follow others' lead.

Such rules are for art's sake. A quiet intermediary pause enables the artists to compose themselves for what comes next. And the silence following the consummation of a set piece produces a delicious moment of suspended drama before the audience responds.

Glyndebourne

The interval at the Glyndebourne opera is what many people go there for. This glorious location, near Lewes in East Sussex, is the setting not only for outstanding operatic productions but also for matchless scenery among which to picnic. Black tie is worn, with women in long evening dress, the seventy-five minutes between acts is just sufficient to unpack the hamper, slice through the smoked salmon and venison, dunk the bubbly in the lake to cool and enjoy your tuck in an atmosphere of sheer enchantment. Tickets are hard to come by; most are snapped up by members of the five thousand-strong Glyndebourne Festival Society.

Concerts

You need not dress formally, just smartly, for most classical concerts. Arriving late is not on; you will certainly be barred from entrance until the end of a piece.

Extraneous noise is anathema to classical concert audiences. Rustling paper, whispering or – heaven forbid – humming along will engender hostility from all around. Nor is there any sympathy for coughers and wheezers.

Applause between movements does not demonstrate laudable enthusiasm; it is either ignorance or a disregard for the needs of the conductor and musicians to re-settle themselves. When an audience seems to be austere and unappreciative, one should keep one's nerve and not feel obliged to express continual gratitude on everyone else's behalf. If unsure, you should wait until the majority of the audience clap.

It is advisable to reserve drinks for the interval if you don't want to face long queues and short tempers. Book cabs for the end of the performance to avoid similar problems.

Theatre

Not only does London's West End brim with theatres, but there are many outstanding outer London and provincial companies all offering splendid opportunities for business entertaining – not to mention sponsorship.

The best seats are in the front ten rows of the stalls or in the front five of the dress circle. Boxes may be prestigious, but in many theatres – short of grasping one's valued client by the ankles as he leans out for a better look – they do not give a full view of the stage.

As above, organise interval drinks before the show starts, and if possible reserve a table in the bar. Many shows end at about 10pm, so it is a reasonable idea to suggest – and then book – supper to follow.

Galleries

Sharing an invitation with a client to the opening of an art exhibition is a smart move. These can be cosy and prestige-laden affairs: an exclusive invited guest list, free wine and buffet, bright conversation, great snob value and the opportunity for the ladies to wear their more outrageous numbers.

In some of London's smarter galleries, too, there is a chance to do some celebrity spotting. Although the practice may rankle with the seasoned *boulevardier*, it can be a thrill for the out-of-towner who will enjoy dropping a heavy name or two on his return to home base.

You should arrive on time, as many contemporary exhibition openings begin with a speech by the artist. The catalogue will contain background information on him, which is worth reading in case you are introduced and wish to say something meaningful.

The atmosphere will vary according to the gallery, but on such occasions you should be prepared for behaviour ranging from the intense and cryptic to the colourful and bizarre.

Charity galas

These occasions can take the form of a concert, a ball, a cabaret or a dinner. They are the most prestigious, glittering and expensive occasions of the social calendar and may be attended by the royal, the renowned, the rich and the rude.

There is a London gala circuit attended by the same people night after night, so such occasions can be elitist and cliquey. If you are unconnected, it is more comfortable to go with your own clique – four people at least.

One wears the smartest of evening wear and accessories and should be equally lavish in one's generosity to the cause. Many people tend to behave in an unattractively ostentatious or flashy manner when contributing money on these occasions. Those who give from the heart are the quietest about it.

The Queen's Award

This is one of the royal events which you do not wait to be invited to or sponsored for. You nominate yourself.

There are two categories: the Queen's Award for Export Achievement and the Queen's Award for Technological Achievement. The Queen grants the awards on the advice of the Prime Minister and an advisory committee made up of representatives from industry, commerce, the trade unions and government departments.

In the export category the winning criterion is 'substantial and sustained increase in export earnings to a level which is outstanding for the products or services concerned and for the size of the applicant unit's operations'. In the technology sector it is 'a significant advance, leading to increased efficiency, in the application of technology to a production or development process in British industry or the production for sale of goods which incorporate new and advanced technological qualities'.

Application forms and explanatory literature are obtainable from The Queen's Awards Office (see Useful Addresses).

The awards are made annually on the Queen's personal birthday, 21 April. For five years thereafter the company can display the Award emblem on company flags, stationery, livery etc.

Their company having been chosen for an Award, three members of each winning firm go – in business suits – to meet the Queen and the Duke of Edinburgh at an official ceremony at Buckingham Palace. There they will be presented with the trophy and have a brief conversation with Their Majesties.

As always, the Queen is addressed as 'Your Majesty', subsequently 'Ma'am' (pronounced 'Mam') and the Duke as 'Your Royal Highness', then 'Sir'. The royal couple will have been briefed about the company's achievements. They ask the questions, and steer and terminate the conversation. (See also p. 122.)

At a mutually convenient time after that date the Queen's representative, the Lord Lieutenant of the relevant county, will attend the company itself for a second ceremony with documents and regalia. A jolly good lunch or buffet should be organised to receive him. Following that, as many of the workforce as possible should attend the presentation ceremony.

Playing golf

Contrary to popular legend and executive pleading, a golf course is not the best setting in which to hack out business deals. It is a verdant arena better suited to building relationships and for creative thinking. Three hours or so strolling together in pleasant surroundings is conducive to formulating new ideas. Deals, if they must be concluded, are best left till after the eighteenth hole. Company handicap tournaments, too, are excellent opportunities for executives and their spouses to establish closer relationships with their opposite numbers.

As with purely recreational golf, if you are an inept or inexperienced player you should not suggest a game with a mustard-keen, low-handicap client. Thrashing a ball in assorted directions and disappearing for long periods to retrieve it is an imposition on his patience and goodwill.

'Good etiquette demands listening more than you speak; observing before reacting . . . it's no coincidence that exactly the same rules apply in effective business practice.'

ANGELA HEYLIN, Chairman (sic) and Chief Executive of Charles Barker Holdings (one of the world's top advertising agencies).

Chapter 18

ADDRESSING DIGNITARIES

IF YOU are representing your company you may well meet titled people and other dignitaries, and it is as well to know how to address them. Writing to such people was dealt with in Chapter 5, and addressing royalty in Chapter 17. Here's how to address a whole host of other people who have an official rank or status.

Dukes and below

Order of seniority:

- Royal duke (direct relative of the queen)
- Duke
- Marquess
- Earl
- Viscount
- Baron
- Baronet
- Knight.

At formal affairs, royal dukes and duchesses are presented with their full titles: 'His Royal Highness the Duke of Somewhere'. They are addressed as 'Your Royal Highness' initially, thereafter 'Your Grace' or 'Sir/Ma'am'.

Lesser dukes are presented as 'The Duke of Somewhere' and are addressed as 'Your Grace' or 'Duke'. Their wives are addressed as 'Duchess', then 'Your Grace' or 'Ma'am'.

Dowager duchesses (widows) are presented as 'Duchess Somebody'.

In writing they should be called 'The Dowager Duchess of Somewhere'. They should be addressed as 'Duchess'.

The sons and daughters of dukes are Lords and Ladies. Depending on their age, their title is used with their first name, i.e. 'Lord/Lady Firstname.'

Marquesses (or marquis) and marchionesses, viscounts and viscountesses, barons and baronesses, and earls and countesses are addressed by their titles or as 'Your Lordship/Ladyship' and 'Lord/Lady Somebody'.

The sons of marquesses are 'Your Lordship' or 'Lord Somebody'. The children of earls are 'The Hon. Somebody Somebody' but are addressed without titles.

A baronet and a knight are 'Sir Firstname'; their wives are 'Lady Surname'.

A dame – the female equivalent of a knight – is normally addressed as 'Dame Firstname'; her husband has no corresponding title.

Courtesy titles

Mayoralty

London, Belfast, Cardiff, Dublin and York all have lord mayors. They are presented as 'The Rt Hon. Lord Mayor of Somewhere'. They and all other lord mayors are addressed as '(My) Lord Mayor'.

A mayor is addressed as 'Your Worship', 'Mayor Somebody' or 'Mr Mayor'. His wife (or daughter if she fulfils the official function) is presented as 'Lady Mayoress'.

Lady Mayors are also known as mayoresses and addressed as 'Your Worship', 'Mayor Somebody' or Madam Mayor', and sometimes still as 'Mr Mayor'.

Aberdeen, Dundee, Edinburgh and Glasgow all have Lord Provosts. They are addressed as 'Provost', 'My Lord', 'Your Lordship' or 'Mr Chairman' – or the female equivalents.

Aldermen and councillors are addressed as such.

The clergy

The Pope is addressed as 'Your Holiness'.

Cardinals are addressed by title (i.e. 'Cardinal') or as 'Your Eminence'.

Anglican and Roman Catholic bishops are addressed by title or as 'My Lord'.

Most other clergy are addressed by their titles, e.g. Rabbi, Canon, Monsignor, Vicar, Father Somebody, etc.

133

Politicians

The Prime Minister is addressed by title.

Government ministers are addressed as 'Minister'.

MPs are addressed by name.

Further reference

The most comprehensive source of titles and forms of address can be found in *Debrett's Correct Form* edited by Patrick Montague-Smith, published by Webb and Bower.

Chapter 19

WARDROBE AND GROOMING

PICTURE yourself in the clothes you wear for work. Better still, take a look in a full-length mirror. Check your shape, your colouring and your character. Then ask yourself what your clothes and your grooming do for you in each of those three categories. If the answer is 'nothing', you may decide they don't do any harm either and leave it at that.

That would be a pity. All surveys confirm that a person's business look makes an important impression on colleagues and clients. And many middle-ranking British businessmen are found lagging behind their crisper, better-groomed and more relaxed-looking European and American colleagues.

Our businesswomen do rather better, although some complain of the difficulty of achieving a balance between femininity and formality.

Before you tear yourself away from that mirror, it may be worth checking your current image. Does your outfit still match your job? For example, a manifestly casual look may be inappropriate if you have recently been promoted to a more responsible position.

Company style

A company usually has its own traditions and level of fashion. These relate to its field of activity and what has been established by its senior executives. If you are a new recruit and unsure what to wear, the simple rule is to follow their lead to start with.

Only arty organisations – advertising, publishing, certain areas of television – can get away with the 'havoc' look of shabby jeans, floppy tops etc. Even here, if you really don't look good in blue denim and sweaters, a good tactic is to dress smartly so as to stand out.

Cost

Making your business look work for you is a worthwhile and effective investment, and not necessarily an expensive one.

> There is one rule that covers every element of the business wardrobe, be it clothing, shoes, accessories or grooming: never go cheap.

Cheap clothes are usually copies of expensive ones, but not made in the material they were designed for. As a result they hang badly and deteriorate quickly. There is rarely a need for you to boast how cheap a new bargain outfit was. As it gets tatty and worn it will say so on your behalf.

But don't go to the other extreme: between tat and clothes costing hundreds of pounds are those obtainable from good department and chain stores, on credit if necessary. And for the patient, there are bargains in the twice-yearly sales. Good-quality clothes are an important investment. They will last a long time when cared for, and will probably be worth altering to stay in tune with fashion.

Consultancy

If cost is not a prime consideration, you may wish to get expert advice on your wardrobe. An image consultant can be engaged to analyse your physical attributes and to recommend precisely the clothes and accessories to enhance them.

You will be told which colours best compliment you. Also, those which contrast and combine well on you, for occasions when you are seeking to make extra impact. Your character, personality and job will be appraised and a style recommended. This will take into consideration not only what looks good on you, but also what you enjoy wearing. The advice may lead you along hitherto unthought of and more flattering sartorial avenues.

Best of all, you won't be told to go away and lose weight before you can wear what would best suit you. Consultants worth their title are too canny for that. You will simply be shown how to make the best of your present condition.

Magazines

These are a good source of new ideas for the less than super-rich. But there is a pitfall into which many topple by not recognising that photographic models are built differently from ordinary folk – usually higher and narrower, and often much trimmer. And clothes don't always fit *them* properly, either. Fashion shoots involve hidden forests of pins, and mountains of tape, padding and clamping.

The best advice is to stay clear of the latest fashions if they don't actually suit you. Buy only what *you* look good and comfortable in. Your aim should be to create a style of your own. Clothes are an expression of a person's self-image. Check that yours express self-confidence and well-organised resources.

> 'I've always known that the way you dress, whether you're a man or a woman, has a huge influence on your self-confidence and on the way people relate to you. Now that I'm designing for the corporate field as well, I'm even more convinced! When a person knows he or she is looking good, it enhances their business performance beyond measure.'
>
> ELIZABETH EMANUEL, fashion designer.

Suits

A business wardrobe for either sex should include at least three suits.

A practical balance for men is one summer-weight suit, lightish in colour but not bright; one darkish winter-weight suit, and one mid-weight suit in mid-grey or with a light stripe.

Businesswomen's outfits are more versatile. Two or three of them can be chosen for their matching or complementary cut and colour so they can be mixed: jackets with other skirts and dresses; skirts with other tops.

Women's trousers

Whether or not a woman wears trousers is a question of company style. If they are acceptable, then they obviously should be elegant, well-cut and made of good fabric. Above all, they should suit the wearer – and that's the rub.

Trousers do not suit those with oversized behinds and short legs (the same goes for men, although they have little choice in the matter; however a cunningly tailored jacket is an adequate disguise). Women with flat behinds and long legs look good in trousers, but they look even smarter in any number of styles of skirts.

. . . and coats

Coats for business should be of quiet design, long enough to cover dresses and large enough to accommodate shoulder padding comfortably. Anoraks are okay if you ski to work.

Shoes

Among the business prejudices concerning shoes are the following:

- A woman who wears skimpy shoes with very high heels is not properly job-motivated. Also, she marks floors with them
- Men with scruffy shoes, or who wear brown shoes with a grey suit, lack leadership qualities
- Trainers are for eccentrics or messengers.

Then there are the more useful tenets:

- Men's shoes should be black or brown, or minor variations thereof. Light grey and beige are best avoided
- Shoe trees are an excellent investment and can make footwear last years longer
- Shabby, scuffed or unpolished shoes wreck the look of an otherwise impeccable outfit
- Cheap shoes look that way after day one.

. . . and socks

Men's socks should cover more than just the ankle; bare white flesh flashing beneath trouser bottoms is not an attractive sight. They should be plain and quiet or with a muted pattern, and not 100 per cent ordinary nylon because it is non-absorbent and becomes uncomfortable and smelly.

Jewellery

Cascades of chunky, bright junk jewellery festooned about the person is all right for the young, but it shows a lack of sophistication on the middle-aged. Jewellery, junk or genuine, should be worn sparingly.

If a man wears ear-rings, bracelets, neck chains or big rings for business, he must accept the risk of alienating, and perhaps confusing, some members of the conservative business community.

Grooming

Many people are sensitive to the slightest hint of body odour. So when working in confined spaces in proximity to others, use a deodorant. When wearing perfume or after-shave, it should be supplemented by an odourless deodorant or one containing the same perfume. And remember that too much of any perfume or after-shave – however good and expensive – is off-putting.

Products containing cheap scents should be used only to freshen toilets and carpets. Working next to someone who wears a cheap perfume is an unpleasant, almost toxic, experience. One of the reasons why good fragrances, and products containing them cost more is that they go further and last longer and are often as economic as the kind of bargain jumbo-sized deodorant that almost blows your arm off and is possibly even worse than the odour it was meant to counteract.

Well-groomed hair is important for both men and women. Women don't usually need prompting, but men must remember to go regularly to the hairdresser – scruffy hair does not go unnoticed from above. And hair should always look fresh and clean. Excess nose and ear hair should also regularly be cropped away – some people find it repellent. Moustaches and beards should be kept trim and should never proclaim what one had for lunch.

Good grooming means being 100 per cent impeccable. So before rushing out, take a minute to inspect yourself from top to toe. Check that your hems are not letting you down, that no buttons are missing, that your grand turnout is unblemished by stains, flecks of dust, dandruff, stray hairs, grubby shoes, razor cuts, food particles between the teeth and gapping zips.

A personal grooming kit tucked away in the desk will prove useful. Keep in it:

- clothes brush
- toothbrush and toothpaste
- nail file
- nail brush
- tissues
- deodorant
- comb/brush
- cologne

- breath freshener
- scissors
- neutral shoe shiner
- sewing kit.

Women should add:

- spare tights or stockings
- make-up basics
- sanitary items.

Men should add:

- razor or battery shaver.

Evening wear

A man's clothes for a formal evening cocktail party or dinner are pretty simple: dark lounge suit, black shoes and socks, sober shirt and tie.

For that kind of function a woman can wear either a dark or print dress, sparse costume jewellery and evening pumps and carry a small handbag. Alternatively an evening suit with either skirt or trousers can be worn.

'Black-tie' evening parties are simple for men: evening dress (dinner suit), including a white handkerchief arranged in points in the breast pocket, bow tie and discreet cuff links. Preparation becomes slightly more intricate when a self-tied bow tie is worn but the effect is considerably more debonair. Make sure the fabric of the bow tie matches that of the suit.

Before donning a frilly shirt or cummerbund, it is well worth checking whether or not they are in fashion. At the time of writing, neither is seen on the stylish bon viveur.

Braces not belts are worn with dinner jackets.

For women, outfits can range from short to full-length dresses with matching evening bag and evening slippers, to sleek blouses and skirts or slinky trousers, embellished with sparse formal costume jewellery or genuine articles.

Women beware

Plunging necklines and slit-to-the-hip skirts may be fine for formal parties with friends. Such outfits are not appropriate for business social occasions. Long gloves are for very formal occasions only. Finally, be careful of the effect of wearing conspicuous jewellery; it should be worn to enhance one's appearance, not to provoke awe or envy.

> It does not look good to touch up your make-up at meetings, in mixed company or during meals. Always retire to the ladies' room to do so.

Very formal wear

For international balls and equally lavish affairs, 'white-tie' is often stipulated for men. This includes tails – stiff shirt, wing collar and stud, waistcoat, white piqué bow tie, black patent leather shoes and white gloves. For big budget weddings one should verify what apparel is required; it could be morning dress and top hat. All the aforementioned outfits can be hired.

These are the occasions for women to wear their most lavish gowns. Once upon a time they would have worn furs on top; to do so nowadays may invite abuse.

> Everything a man needs for an important occasion – be it a black-tie or white-tie do, or a smart wedding – can be hired. Women, too, now often hire ball dresses. Book early to get the pick of the bunch.

Travelling

Hopping from place to place and country to country is easier when travelling light. The secret is again clothes-coordination in cut and colour. Choose uncrushable fabrics, as long as they are not too warm for hot countries. There are other factors to consider when travelling further afield.

Heading eastwards

In Japan (see also Chapters 21 and 22) and some Arab countries (Chapters 23 and 24), be sure your hosiery is in good condition as you may have to remove your shoes when you enter a holy shrine or people's homes.

In the Republic of China, don't wear white – it is a sign of mourning.

In most Arab countries, women should wear long-sleeved tops and below-the-knee skirts and dresses; never trousers.

When sightseeing in many Catholic countries, women's arms, shoulders and heads must be covered – so take a cover-up. Skirts should be below the knee.

Further sartorial pitfalls and suggestions are included in most travel guides to foreign countries. Don't take off without reading one.

Chapter 20

STRICTLY WOMEN

ACCORDING to the working philosophies of a number of top female business executives, for a woman to succeed she does not need to become a surrogate man. They maintain that women have qualities men do not possess, and that women are truly successful when they conduct themselves in a way that maintains their femininity without surrendering business ground.

But the battleground is not an even one. Among the humps are many men's fragile egos. Some women will manoeuvre their way around them without much trouble. Others will trample all over them, and feel aggrieved if they are accused of bitchiness. As with men, aggression (in contrast to assertiveness, which can be a legitimate business attitude) makes life more difficult for oneself and for others.

There are, of course, as many types of women as there are men. Some women's sexuality is more conspicuous, so their experiences and attitudes are different from those who consider gender to be irrelevant to business performance and therefore strive to neutralise it.

The feminist movement has focused attention on some appalling sexual injustices and has helped to shift the balance dramatically. But it seems to have failed to resolve one fundamental aspect of human behaviour: the respect each gender demonstrates for the other.

Attitude

In most companies simple issues of etiquette, such as whether or not men open doors or stand up for women and so on, are muddled through. What often remains decidedly unsatisfactory is the attitude with which these courtesies are observed or ignored.

Some men mistakenly feel that their female colleagues lose their entitlement to courtesy by accepting equal conditions and pay. More insultingly, politeness is exaggerated and used as a weapon to put a woman 'in her place', while women often err by spurning genuine gestures of courtesy from men. The unhappy conflict continues.

Sexual attitudes are changing, but the change is slow, particularly among many of the older generation. Those male-oriented practices that do not respect women's equal place in business are often based on defensive and other fearful attitudes. These are infuriating, but the most effective way of eliminating them is not by open warfare. A more subtle approach, albeit requiring enormous self-control, may prove more effective and less debilitating.

Among the cosy but sage maxims that support this view, and also preserve good business behaviour, are:

- Women who feel they must emulate men in order to succeed should consider emulating only those who are considerate and compassionate

- When there is mutual respect for the like and complementary abilities of both sexes, everyone gains.

'To be tough is one thing. To be a bitch is another. A bitch is petty, spiteful and insecure. Tough is to have your priorities right. I am tough, but in no way am I a bitch.'

STEVIE FREDERICK, electronics magnate, as quoted in *The Business Amazons* by LEAH HERTZ, published in 1986 by Deutsch.

Who pours the coffee?

If no one offers, then the most obvious answer is the person nearest the pot. Sometimes, though, it is deliberately placed nearest a woman, it being unconsciously taken for granted that she'll do it.

If the woman doesn't wish to be 'mum' yet again, she should find an excuse to shift it – for example to spread her papers on the table. She should move the pot to a neutral position on the table and not mention it again. Or she should serve herself, and shove the whole tray, if manageable, on to the next person, so a self-service pattern is established.

Some women actually enjoy providing this service. (Yes, they do!) And so long as they can do so without losing status, why not? Furthermore, the ritual can be turned neatly to the pourer's advantage. Handing round refreshments is one way of making personal contact with the entire gathering. An informal word and smile as it is dispensed can establish a useful personal relationship. Additionally, it can provide a strategic advantage: the opportunity to check on everyone's operating status before the meeting has even started, e.g. 'Do you take sugar, Fred? . . . How's the budget proposal going?' etc. And remember, if the coffee is distributed with a confident and self assured air, and not subserviently, it implies being in charge.

Neglect

It may sound obvious to some, but it is worth re-emphasising that a woman should be accepted purely for the job she does: her contribution to her company and department. If a woman is not offered the same training and promotion opportunities as the men, she should consider taking action in one of two ways. Either she should talk to the boss and have the position remedied, or she should take her skills elsewhere. She should not sit and simmer and allow resentment to affect her performance and business relationships. Her company will learn its bitter lesson eventually, but rather than waiting around for the penny to drop she should consider looking around for a better position.

Women vs women

Some women hate others of their sex to be successful. They can be even more discourteous to one another than men are to them. One senior woman executive was quoted as saying she sometimes had to go so far as to pretend to be a secretary in order to get cooperation from other women in her company!

Many women who have struggled to the top, having once been treated as menials, fall into the trap of treating their own secretaries badly.

Women will usually help their oppressed sisters, but there are those who are reluctant to lend a hand to females in more senior positions. Whatever their reasons – and jealousy is sometimes one of them – this attitude seriously retards the cause of sex equality. Women executives still have to make considerable personal sacrifices to compete with men, so they need all the understanding and support they can get from other women.

Women as managers

Although women managers are becoming a more established fact of life in many companies, the criteria for behaviour are unfairly balanced. If, for example, they issue orders in the way male managers do, people may react on the lines of 'who does she think she is?'. Women staff are rather less inclined than men to confront such problems; instead they may bottle up their feelings of resentment.

The longer a manager allows this resentment to exist the more damaging it will become. An effective way to deal with it and to improve her lines of communication is to invite her senior staff members – male and female – into her office, individually or in groups of no more than four, to discuss any problems they have in this area. She should take that opportunity to express what she expects of them, and to bring out into the open any difficulties they have in relation to her procedures and intentions.

In their turn, individual members of her staff who have problems dealing with the way she operates, should consider asking for a private interview in order to talk it through. Things may not change, but at least communication should be substituted for resentment and rancour. See also Chapter 3.

Incumbents vs women

Certain business areas can be difficult and unpleasant for a woman to work in, particularly those with male traditions. Many incumbents resent – and fear – incursion by women; some even coin infantile expressions to try to demean them – for example, 'trouts' for females who work in the city.

One rarely overcomes such attitudes by argument, and certainly not by performance. Theirs is a fight for lost citadels. The anger and resentment this induces in women is understandable, but such emotional responses would be helped by an understanding of why such behaviour exists. It could be, as certain clinical psychologists maintain, that men are driven less by the need to be successful than by the fear of being seen as failures.

When entering the business arena, a woman must simply keep her own counsel, behave respectfully towards those who behave respectfully towards her, and maintain a strictly business attitude to the less considerate. It might be too idealistic to suggest that she will change men's attitudes through demonstrating equal competence and dignified deportment. That in effect may be even more threatening. Nor should she necessarily be a martyr to time, by contributing to a slowly maturing culture. It is a more expedient strategy for the proficient woman to work her way up on to higher levels as soon as she is able.

146

Gender not sex

Using sexual charms in business is dangerous and self-destructive. Furthermore, they are unlikely to work beyond the age of forty (all right, fifty).

Coyness and titillation may be okay one-to-one, but they will cause embarrassment in a boardroom.

An attractive woman shouldn't be too chummy when meeting a male colleague for the first time; some men confuse being friendly with being seductive. In large corporations, a male colleague should be greeted with a handshake, not a kiss. Kissing implies an intimacy which may be resented by others less favoured.

> Dressing like a sex-bomb prevents a woman from being taken seriously. But one should not deliberately become a frump. There is an elegant way of dressing which maintains dignity without detracting from gender.

Being patronised

Smiling is the crucial weapon in the battle against being patronised. It works, even though stopping it from bending into a leer can sometimes be very difficult. When men say 'Try to understand', a woman should force herself to smile brightly and say something on the lines of 'Well, I'll try.' When they say 'Thank you, dear', she should respond with a smile and, perhaps: 'It's a pleasure, love.' And to the regular charge of 'Is it that time of the month?' the reply could be 'No, just that time of the day,' and a smile.

Business travel

Travelling and staying in hotels alone is not much fun for anyone. For a woman, it involves a number of obvious additional hazards. Seventy per cent of business women who responded to a national survey in 1990, said they took meals in their rooms when travelling to avoid problems. There are ways of alleviating the stresses and embarrassments that are currently part of the travelling businesswoman's lot.

- Some women tip the reception staff when they arrive, to motivate special care and attention

147

- Wherever possible, carry your briefcase with you so you are classified by fellow residents as a professional business person

- Use room service rather than run the gauntlet of tipsy sales reps in hotel restaurants

- Don't drink alone in the bar; it signals availability

- Wear a business suit, rather than a cocktail dress, when dining alone

- Book a corner table, so you can observe rather than be exposed

- Work on some papers between courses, to consolidate your working image and to help cover any shyness

- If a man comes over and sits with you uninvited and unwanted, simply tell him to leave as you want to be on your own. Then ignore him and any conversation he tries to make. If he refuses to budge, call the waiter over and ask him to show the man back to his own table

- If the man is attractive to you and charmingly asks you to join him, you can accede – but just for a drink as you have so much work to do during the meal

- If things warm up and a second drink is called for, insist on paying for it so no indebtedness is incurred. If you then wish to accept his suggestion to dine together, it is prudent not to leave the hotel to do so

- After dinner, you're on your own.

'One of the biggest concerns women express in letters to *Cosmo* is how to be assertive without appearing aggressive. With increasing numbers of them now in managerial positions, it is crucial that they don't intimidate and inhibit their colleagues and employees, male *and* female. One of the keys is to be firm whilst displaying courtesy and respect – that respect is invariably reciprocated.'

MARCELLE D'ARGY SMITH, Editor of *Cosmopolitan*.

Forbidden business behaviour

Men can get away with some kinds of behaviour that are not acceptable in women. This is unfair and can be frustrating, so to avoid extra embarrassment a woman sometimes needs extra behavioural skills. Here are some of the areas that need careful navigation:

- When arguing, keep a check on your voice so it doesn't become shrill. (Men, on the other hand, are allowed to whine)

- Shouting, screaming or becoming emotional will label you a shrew. (Men can get worked up about anything, lose their tempers, apologise and everyone is expected to forgive and forget)

- Don't become part of a segregated female clique which gossips about men behind their backs. (Men are seemingly permitted to stand in groups making personal remarks about women as they pass)

- If you are a boss, don't be bossy, but delegate work tactfully. (Tyrannical male bosses are simply doing their job 'dynamically')

- Don't get loaded at lunch – a tipsy, dishevelled woman executive weaving her way to her desk makes a pitiful, even scandalous sight. (It is 'necessary' for men to drink plenty at lunch to cement relationships with clients.)

Women's networks

Old boy networks exist for the welfare and advancement of men. It is difficult, if not impossible, for a woman to break into most of them. So if you can't join them, establish one of your own.

A large number of effective women's business organisations have been set up and have flourished in recent years. There are many to choose from. Their meetings and functions cover general and specific business issues as well as the problems of women working in a male environment.

Some of the organisations that provide support, encouragement, advice and inspiration for women in business are listed in Useful Addresses.

Part III

FOREIGN ETIQUETTE

Chapter 21

JAPANESE BUSINESS ETIQUETTE

JAPAN is different from any other market in the world, and if you wish to do business with the Japanese there is no alternative but to abide by their unique code of business etiquette.

Most of their major companies are run on strictly formal lines. Things are starting to change as the younger, post-1950s' generation begins to make its mark on the business world. Younger managers often have different values and are less ritualistic in their business conduct. But for some years yet, power will be wielded and procedures controlled by the traditional establishment.

Established Japanese companies do not like to operate on the basis of one-off deals: their approach is to establish long-term partnerships. They are uncomfortable doing business with strangers, so it is important to create mutual trust and understanding. That is achieved through the behaviour of your company's representatives. If their manners and attitude are considered disrespectful, business relationships will be seriously jeopardised.

> The success of a partnership with a Japanese company is directly related to the strength of inter-personal relationships.

Organisations offering advice to companies wanting to trade with Japan can be found in the list of Useful Addresses.

Respect

The basis of Japanese etiquette is respect – for individuals, companies, ideals and methodologies. Respect is demonstrated in every aspect of good behaviour. For example, when a Japanese agrees to allow you to pay for lunch, he is respecting your right and ability to do so.

Before a business relationship can be formed, one must get to know and trust a person. Few established companies will do business with those whose status and reliability is unproved.

Personal ranking is very important. Any action which indicates disrespect for a person's position is considered unforgivable and will seriously threaten a business relationship. If the Japanese provide top-level management they expect to do business with the equivalents from the other company. A Japanese chief executive may refuse to deal with an assistant CE from another company. Only where another company is highly ranked will they agree to their people meeting executives with a lower rank.

Paradoxically, they would not be flattered by a company sending too high an executive to a meeting. Their customs are based on tradition and not on ego; such tactics might make them feel pressurised and cause them to pull back.

Just as boss meets boss, lower ranks are looked after by their equivalents, in terms of both business and social activities.

Information

From the very beginning, the Japanese will require copious amounts of printed information about your company. It is absolutely essential that you supply it, in detail. Failure to do so will delay or even terminate negotiations. The information you supply will be passed through to their colleagues and superiors as well as to the Ministry of International Trade and Industry (MITI).

You are perfectly entitled to request and receive similar information from them. In some cases, it might be considered negligent and inept not to do so. Just so long as it is asked for with respect and without causing offence: 'Our board of directors always needs a complete file on all our business partners' is the right kind of thing to say.

Making initial contacts

Appointments should be made before arriving in the country. Failure to do so will incur long delays.

Large Japanese companies have a number of executives dealing with foreign trade, and it can take time to identify the appropriate person dealing with your area of business. Japanese business people dislike unsolicited approaches. It is far better to be introduced by a mutual contact such as a bank or other respected business associate. If a personal recommendation cannot be arranged, a letter of introduction is essential.

Introductions

When being introduced, a Japanese businessman will present his card (see below) and state his surnames, followed by the first name. When a Westerner introduces himself, however, he should give his first name then surname, in the normal manner. Bowing (see next page) is also part of the ritual of introduction.

When introducing their colleagues, the Japanese attach 'san' to the end of a name; this is a courtesy suffix equivalent to our Mr, Miss or Mrs. One does not, however, add 'san' to one's own name – that would be presumptuous. You should call them Mr Somebody, or Surname-san. They will indicate when the time has come for first names. They will call you Mr Somebody or Surname-san. If you have established the appropriate relationship, they will call you First name-san.

The Japanese like to present gifts to important visitors. You may like to exchange the compliment. The full ritual is covered in Chapter 22.

Business cards

Commercial printing has to be one of Japan's jackpot professions. Briefcases are crammed to the seams with business cards which are dispensed like confetti.

> Unlike the bygone British custom of gingerly handing one business card to be shared by everyone at the end of a meeting, the Japanese propel them in all directions the moment you are introduced.

Cards are also exchanged at informal affairs, such as cocktail parties.

It is discourteous not to return the gesture. The visiting businessman should ensure he has an ample supply to hand out deftly on the many occasions they are required throughout the day. When dealing with a big company, one can easily distribute fifty cards in a day. Everyone in the business circle should be given one. To leave anyone out – excluding perhaps the lift operator – may give offence.

Fortunately most companies print their cards with English translations. You must return the courtesy and have your card printed in their language, handing them over Japanese side up.

Exchanging cards is a practical courtesy that not only aids identification, but is essential to the Japanese in establishing everyone's status and position. Titles should be carefully translated, as they may not have equivalents.

When a card is handed to a person of very superior rank, it is proferred with both hands.

The card should be read as soon as it is handed to you. One should enquire about pronunciation if necessary. Here again, the Japanese surname is placed before the given name. Cards should be placed in front of you and left there, not put straight into pocket or briefcase.

Providing a short, respectful introductory letter in Japanese that outlines your company and your position is also very worthwhile. This should be given along with your card and your bow.

Bowing

In Japan, bowing the head is a mark of mutal respect. In regular business relationships, the subordinate person will bow slightly lower and slightly longer. On average, the head is bowed two or three times. The hands are placed flat on the thighs, fingers straight, eyes lowered.

It has been estimated that there are twenty-six combinations of depth and quantity of bows. But the canniest way of establishing what is required is to follow the lead of the person you are greeting. If he is the client, or of superior rank, allow him to stop bowing before you do, if possible.

When you are first introduced to people, the bows should be more pronounced. The same goes for the first bows of the day.

A handshake does not come naturally to an unwesternised Japanese. If one is proffered, it should follow the bow. The grip should be gentle.

Professional translation

Translators experienced in business communication are invaluable. They not only translate but should filter out the words and expressions that the Japanese might find alien or offensive.

A translator will be expert in Japanese prevarication. This technique is not normally employed to frustrate, but used to maintain harmony. If this seems over-defensive, consider the fatal consequences when one artless British businessman kept employing the idiom: 'You must be joking!' They weren't – they seldom do – and he found himself shut out. Even a tempered 'under no circumstances . . .' can be too strong.

A good translator will also adjust uses of dangerous phrases like 'It is very difficult', which in Japanese conveys 'Absolutely not'. He would massage that phrase appropriately, couch it in some reflective silence and pass it on as 'I really must consider this very carefully. Please allow me to let you know tomorrow.'

He will also modify the word 'No', which is hardly ever heard in Japanese companies, except by people accustomed to more direct western discourse. The Japanese on the whole favour moderating expressions like 'If you think so.'

Women

Businesswomen have had a tough time being accepted by the Japanese commercial community. They are frequently an isolated class, and are rarely invited into the men's social circle. However, the signs are that women are becoming more important and powerful in business, particularly in the service industries.

> The Japanese are accustomed to seeing women in subservient roles. They are particularly uncomfortable if a woman executive tries to act in a masculine and aggressive manner.

A foreign woman wishing to do business with long-established and traditionally male-dominated Japanese companies is advised to employ a distinctly soft manner. This may help to counter their stereotypical view of European and American women as imperious and impertinent. A woman who shows an open interest in the Japanese language and culture will help to overcome the typically hypersensitive Japanese attitude to females in business.

Meetings

The first meeting is usually for preliminary observation: Japanese shadow boxing. No apparent progress on a proposition may be made at all. They will just observe and listen. They may not even broach the reason for getting together in the first place. Once again, you should not try to rush things or to take control. You should follow their lead and give them the once-over too. It is a valuable custom, a familiarisation process that can also help people become more relaxed in one another's company.

In large companies, seating arrangements are according to rank. The best place in the room is considered to be that furthest from the door – or nearest to the *tokonoma*: an alcove featuring a scroll on which a short poem is written. This position is usually reserved for the principal guest. It should be accepted with grace and appreciation.

Allow yourself to get into a rhythm of negotiation in which time is allowed for deep consideration. Fast answers are not respected, and long silences are normal – they are thinking time. The Japanese appreciate only the decisions that are given due deliberation – even when they are delayed until the following day. This shows that all ramifications have been thoroughly considered. The answer may be the same as you would have given anyway, but you have been seen to give an important issue the respect that it merits.

Every point will be painstakingly discussed. It will be left only when it has been fully aired, resolved and spelled out, with no element left unclear. The benefits flow both ways, as it also gives you your opportunity to politely air worries and reservations and to find out everything you need to know about them. In the end, you may well resolve issues far more thoroughly than would be the case in Europe.

'The first time I made a presentation to the board of a huge multinational Japanese company (now a valued client), I thought I had blown it. Twenty executives stared at me stone-faced. I battled on for 20 minutes with nothing to react to: not a smile, frown or sigh, hardly even a cough. Afterwards, I was almost in despair until one came over and congratulated me on my success. Success!? "Oh yes," he explained. "If we had reacted otherwise to the presentation, *that* would have been a bad sign, indicating lack of respect for your ideas."'

JEFF GALE, Joint Managing Director of PCI (Presentation Communications International).

Negotiating

The Japanese negotiate aggressively, but always with respect and rarely with rancour – personal relationships are the key to business procedures and must not be endangered.

Most Japanese companies are run by management groups. Personal contact should be made and respects paid to everyone with whom one deals. One must get used to being faced by the large numbers of people the company commits to each deal. It's middle management in action. The more people you can bring to interface with them, the better.

Management of Japanese companies is frequently by consensus and across many levels, so decisions may not be taken by your immediate contacts. They may also be based on factors in which you have no involvement. They will always present a united front although someone's head will probably be slightly above the median. His views will be awaited before any of the others express theirs, usually as endorsements.

Japanese negotiating procedures may be frustrating and appear time-consuming, but it is commercial suicide to criticise either the procedures or anyone involved in them. In short, you must be patient and uncritical. You may think you see imperfections in their methods, but you are in no position to disparage them. They believe their way of doing things is best. But then, Japanese business colleagues never contradict one another. Loyalty is fundamental to Japanese business practice.

Once everyone in the decision-making chain has given his careful consideration, and a conclusion reached, the pace changes dramatically. Immediate, fast action is then expected.

Criticism

Loyalty to one's firm must also be reflected in the visitors' behaviour. He must not complain about his own organisation or permit any colleague to do so. Such behaviour is considered despicable; it also indicates flaws in one's organisation and its management. In short, one should never criticise anyone in any way, it is *self*-destructive.

If comment has to be made on perceived flaws, it should be delivered gently and with enormous tact. Air-clearing heart-to-hearts are best avoided. You may feel you are discussing a Japanese colleague's failures in a straightforward and reasonable manner, and certainly his demeanour will not manifest any signs of distress. But in his heart he will be screaming with humiliation and in his head he will be composing the letter that terminates the relationship.

Other negatives

Blatant flattery is not worth trying. Straightforward gushing will create serious embarrassment. The Japanese are not used to it and will consider the person insincere. They are more subtle in paying compliments. Just considering your product is their compliment to you.

Flamboyant behaviour and pressure are also counter-productive. The established Japanese businessman dislikes loud and overtly aggressive people. He admires veracity, integrity and business insight. He likes to do business with experienced, conscientious people who take the trouble to ascertain and *totally* to accommodate his interests.

Continually talking about money and profits for their own sake will not please the traditional Japanese businessman. The older Japanese (though less so the often more materialistic younger generation) are mostly concerned about what the money is used for. They believe that success is important in terms of its value in a wider social context. Among their major preoccupations are the welfare of their workforce (who are generally on lifetime contracts), their competitiveness and other long-term social and economic issues.

> Despite their country's colossal economic success, the Japanese are near the bottom of the world league when it comes to valuing profitability for its own sake.

Information communication

The Japanese write in pictures and graphics, so they are visually sophisticated. Using visual aids in your presentations will go down well.

Equally, they are addicted to the written word and appreciate 'contact report' summaries after meetings. This is a particularly valuable safeguard where two languages are spoken, as it ensures that everyone has the same understanding of what was said and agreed. Your ability to produce reports, summaries and proposals in both English and Japanese is an important criterion in their judgment of you.

Trust

Never display any form of mistrust – they will be deeply offended. Worse still, don't brandish the word 'lawyer' during discussions. This could indicate that you are suspicious of them. It threatens loss of face and could lead to the door closing firmly in yours. Whatever is discussed and agreed is considered binding. The written contract is merely a formality.

159

> In the USA there is one lawyer per 350 people, in the UK one per 800, but in Japan only one per 9000.

Conclusions

Signing a contract – whether for a national telecommunications system or for the supply of saké – will invariably be accompanied by a ceremony. The Japanese enjoy them, with lots of posing for photographs, press statements, smiling guests, hand-shaking and pen-flourishing.

Once an agreement is reached, it is expected that the companies' executives will stay in constant communication. Where possible, visits to one another's plants and offices should be kept up on a regular basis. Failure to do so may imply a lack of interest and commitment to the partnership.

Despite a generally reserved attitude to Westerners, most Japanese like to establish a friendly and continuing relationship with business contacts. For this very reason, it is worthwhile keeping the same people responsible for dealing with them. Should someone's job change, all Japanese counterparts should be informed and the replacement introduced without delay. The new executive should go to Japan at the earliest opportunity, to introduce himself personally and pay his respects.

> Without a regular flow of letters and greeting cards, Japanese businessmen lose interest and consider the relationship as arbitrary and short-term.

Body language

The Japanese businessman is not tactile. Hand-shaking is about as far as he will go. Bear-hugging, patting and arms round shoulders are discomfiting and unwelcome rituals. In short, the Japanese should be given plenty of space. (The rule is even more strict with Japanese women, many of whom are embarrassed by physical contact with Westerners.) The Japanese even stand further apart than Westerners when conversing.

If a business relationship is developing into a more friendly one, they will indicate when shoulder-squeezing, back-patting and the like are acceptable. A foreigner should not try to force the pace.

He should also play it small. In Japan it is considered coarse to take up too much space when sitting or walking or to speak in a loud voice.

Clothes should not be too loud, either. The Japanese admire conservative, well-cut outfits (which may explain why their word for suit is '*sebiro*' – a neat corruption of Savile Row).

- Pointing with the finger is impolite. Rather, turn the hand palm upwards and wave gently toward the object
- Japanese gestures are less expansive than in the West – more wrist flicking than overarm bowling
- Sniffing loudly is perfectly acceptable, but blowing one's nose in a meeting or in public is not
- 'Yes' is indicated by nodding the head. This means the listener agrees, but it is also a polite way of indicating that careful attention is being paid to the speaker's words
- 'No'. The Japanese are reluctant to say 'no', but they will imply it by sharply waving the right hand in front of the face
- 'Excuse me' uses the same gesture as above, but with a repetitive cutting motion
- 'It's me' – point to your nose, not your chest
- 'Shucks' – Japanese women show embarrassment by ducking the head and covering their mouth with their hand. Japanese men don't show embarrassment.

A word or two

A knowledge of at least a few words of Japanese will go a long way. A greeting in Japanese, for example, can be very helpful in relaxing a tense atmosphere among strangers. (To help you with pronunciation, the vowels are generally pronounced as follows: *a* as in 'bar', *e* as in 'ten', *i* as in feet, *o* as in John, and *u* as in dud.)

- 'Good day' = '*Kon-nichi wa*'
- 'Good evening' = '*Konban wa*'
- 'Goodbye' = '*Sayonara*'
- 'No' = '*Iie*' (a word worth forgetting)
- 'Please' (request) = '*Onegai*'
- 'Please' ('Come in' etc.) = '*Dozo*'
- 'Sorry' or 'Excuse me' = '*Gomen nasai*'
- 'Thank you' = '*Arigato gozaimash'ta.*'

161

Chapter 22

JAPANESE SOCIAL CUSTOMS

O N-THE-TOWN business entertaining is an integral part of cementing business relationships in Japan. Entertaining at home is rare, mainly because hideously expensive urban real estate means that even senior executives commute huge distances to work. Those who live centrally rarely have adequate space to hold dinner parties.

It is likely, therefore, that your Japanese hosts will take you out on an itinerary that could include dinner, perhaps a city tour, night clubs, bar and a visit to a traditional theatre – casting you head-first into a dazzling tableau of rites and rituals.

Status and rank

These can be as important in social and private life as in the corporate sphere. It is as well to determine the pecking order at any gathering you attend. The simplest way to do so is by echoing other people's attitudes and behaviour.

> Age is an important factor in traditional Japanese life; older people are usually given superior status. They are never left standing while others sit.

At formal gatherings, most people will not begin to drink or eat before their superiors in age and rank have started. Apart from that, the first thing you may notice is that social equality does not exist in Japan in the way it is understood in the West. Female executives and wives do not customarily accompany the men on business entertainment jaunts. When they do, they normally stay on the sidelines. Often other arrangements will be made for the ladies, normally of a more cultural nature.

The wives have long accepted this treatment. Being married to a traditional Japanese businessman means never having to ask 'When will you be home dear?' He works all the daylight hours, and then goes out all evening with his workmates. She is expected to be waiting, whatever time he arrives, to provide his sustenance. The traditional Japanese businessman is a far cry from the New Man. Thanks to the New Man, however, things are changing gradually. Among other things, many Japanese companies are now organising special functions for *both* sexes!

Men traditionally have a higher cultural standing than women in Japan. For example, the older generation are inclined to precede women through doors. And they rarely surrender a seat to a woman – to do so may imply that there is something wrong with her.

Business lunching

Business lunches are valuable for building relationships, and that's it. In traditional Japanese companies, executives prefer not to work while eating. Lunch is the time to relax and get to know one another, not the time to push forward with negotiating.

One rarely drinks at lunchtime, other than a short in order to deliver a toast: *'Kampai!'*.

Liquid entertainment

If your host asks where you would like to go for evening entertainment, the polite get-out is to ask him to recommend somewhere as he has so much more knowledge than you.

There may be certain rituals involved when you get there, including shoe-removal and floor-sitting. Your host will guide you through this. He will be aware of the Westerner's more chunky thighs, and will arrange for a back rest where no chairs are available.

The odds are that drinking will be included in the itinerary. Drinking is a national pastime, the occasion for traditional Japanese reserve to flow away. Throughout the working day the Japanese businessman keeps his emotional lid tightly capped; when moistened with alcohol, it tends to blast off with surprising velocity. His imperturbable, reserved personality may suddenly become very scrutable indeed. What can emerge is the garrulous and sometimes outrageous Japanese inner man. He will want you to join in the fun.

Females need not apply. It is not done for a woman to turn up and expect to be welcomed as one of the boys. Boozing time in traditional corporate Japan is for men only.

Drinking practice

The fact that this is one of the most expensive countries in the world is reflected in bar tariffs. Drink prices make the average European's head swim: £20 per drink is not unusual, and over £50 for a whisky and soda not unheard of.

Certain conventions should be followed when drinking in polite company. You should never pour your own drink – someone else in your vicinity will do it for you. As they do so, lift your cup or glass, then take a small sip before setting it down. You should pour drinks for others in the same way.

Although whisky abounds, and beer is becoming increasingly popular, saké is the national drink. It is a yellowish-tinted white rice wine, drunk warm. It is bland in taste, with a piquant edge. It slides down easily, like a velvet glove, followed not long afterwards by the iron fist.

Out with the boys

After a formal dinner, you may be invited to a *nijikai* or second party in one of the thousands of drinking places in large Japanese cities. They include *karaoke* – 'empty orchestra' bars where the clients provide the cabaret, singing songs to a pre-recorded or live musical backing. It is worthwhile brushing up on one's own repertoire in case one is called upon to perform. There are also English and American bars, and exclusive clubs – where you will be admitted only if you are accompanied by a member.

And then there are the geisha houses. Authentic geishas are a vanishing species, and only the very top people enjoy their services. The entertainment provided by imitation-geishas in good-class clubs is normally confined to music, singing, dancing and gentle flirtation. The charge for such services is included in the bill. Lower down the scale, for 'geisha' read hostess.

There is generally no tipping for service at bars, restaurants and other such establishments. Allow your host to pay for you on your first visit if he insists. You repay by reciprocating the hospitality on another occasion, or when on your home territory.

Golf is very popular among Japanese executives. Even visitors with massive handicaps should accept invitations to play, as there are few better ways of creating closer business bonds.

Food

Your host will be gratified if you show enthusiasm for his gastronomic culture. This is not a hardship: Japanese food is subtly delicious.

You are best advised not to start groping your way around the à la carte menu. It is wiser to follow your host's advice and choose a set menu.

Most restaurants serve separate courses in individual bowls. They will usually include a favourite dish seen everywhere: raw fish on chunks of rice, known as sushi. Rice and soup bowls each have a lid. It should be removed from the rice and placed on the left; the soup lid should then be removed and placed on the right. A meal normally begins by sampling the rice.

The Japanese are not animal lovers, so they are baffled by moral vegetarianism. It is not advisable to try to convert them or to pit your principles against theirs when out socially.

If your host has recommended the restaurant and selected the food, he will be sensitive to your reactions. Adopt the policy employed by all successful adventurers; don't ask what you are eating. Or do so only if you are prepared to continue whatever the answer.

Learning to use chopsticks will enhance your pleasure and will please your hosts. The first rule of handling them is not to take yourself seriously, or your audience will. They will respond light-heartedly to your mistakes if you do. And they will be happy and complimentary when you succeed.

You may notice your hosts scraping their chopsticks together when they first pick them up. This does not signify joyful anticipation – it is simply to check for splinters. Watch how they eat and follow suit. This may be difficult at first as they will be offering you the first choice of everything.

Be conscious of hygiene: use the serving implements, not your own chopsticks, for communal dishes. If these are not available, reverse your chopsticks and use the clean ends.

'It takes a long time to understand the Japanese culture. But it is essential, because without establishing personal relationships you won't establish business ones.'

MICHAEL PERRY, Director at Unilever and Chairman of the DTI's Japan Trade Advisory Group.

165

Soy sauce is pungent and salty. It is excellent with rice, but as with all condiments one should try the food before deciding on the seasoning. A little soy should be poured on the side of the plate, not all over the food. When being served, it is polite to lift your bowl with both hands.

Gifts

The Japanese enjoy presenting gifts. Business people are often surprised at the trouble they take to find out about a visitor's family and to present gifts especially prepared for spouses and children.

They appreciate receiving them, too. Something small and well considered is most appropriate. It is wise to take with you a selection of such presents as portable gestures of goodwill, and perhaps something a little more elaborate for your principal host. There is every reason for them to incorporate your company's logo. There will probably be many occasions, formal and informal, in which to hand them over. Be sure that they are elegantly wrapped. Many Japanese hotels will provide a lavish wrapping service.

The giving of presents is a subtle art. The giver customarily belittles the gift. The recipient should accept with diffidence, and should not open the gift unless firmly requested to do so. Beware of causing offence by giving too expensive a gift to a business contact – it could be considered a bribe. Don't be too effusive when praising one of your host's possessions, or he may feel obliged to make you a gift of it. Regardless of which of your Japanese associates has been slogging away hardest, the major parting gift always goes to the boss.

If you are in Japan at the beginning of summer or at the end of the year, you may wish to join in the widespread presentation of small gifts between companies and business associates. In the summer the custom is called Ochugen. At year-end it's Oseibo.

Returning gestures

On your first visit to Japan, you will not normally be expected to return your hosts' hospitality. Thereafter, you may wish to invite them to dinner. It may be prudent to do so at your hotel, perhaps in a private banqueting room or at a good table in the hotel restaurant. A speech of thanks to your hosts will also be appreciated.

Never forget to express gratitude to your host for his hospitality while still in Japan. This should be followed up in writing on arrival home.

A word or two more (see p. 161)

The Japanese language is a highly complex one. It has distinct forms of address according to the status of the person being addressed. There are different ways of addressing male superiors and female superiors, male peers and female peers, male inferiors and female inferiors. And there are specific words used when talking to members of the family. Most people abide by these forms of speech and expect to be addressed correctly.

You will not be expected to speak Japanese, but brandishing the following word should go down well before food:

● *'Itadakimas'* = 'Enjoy your meal'

With this one in reserve for emergencies:

● *'Sumimasen'* = 'Sorry' or 'Excuse me'.

Chapter 23

BUSINESS ETIQUETTE IN THE ARAB WORLD

THE following two chapters provide basic guidelines to those general principles of etiquette that are shared by Arab countries in business and socially. See also Useful Addresses.

The Arab World at present consists of the following countries:

- The Democratic and Popular Republic of Algeria
- The State of Bahrain
- The Republic of Djibouti
- The Arab Republic of Egypt
- The Arab Republic of Iraq
- The Hashemite Kingdom of Jordan
- The State of Kuwait
- The Republic of Lebanon
- The Socialist People's Libyan Arab Jamahiriya
- The Islamic Republic of Mauritania
- The Royal Kingdom of Morocco
- The Sultanate of Oman
- The State of Qatar
- The Kingdom of Saudi Arabia
- The Somali Democratic Republic (Somalia)
- The Republic of Sudan

- The Syrian Arab Republic
- The Republic of Tunisia
- The United Arab Emirates
- The Yemen Arab Republic
- The People's Democratic Republic of Yemen.

The area covered by these countries is three times that of Europe, and the total population is over 200 million. The mixture of races, which also includes Berbers, Negroes, Kurds and others, means a variety of cultures and civilisations, but there are two common bonds: membership of the Arab League and, most importantly, Islam, the Muslim religion. Much of the information in this chapter may also be relevant to non-Arab Muslim territories such as Iran, Pakistan, Malaysia and Turkey.

Islam influences virtually every aspect of life in the Arab world. Its authority varies between countries – it is probably at its strictest in Saudi Arabia – but everywhere abuse of its precepts is seldom tolerated.

To a Westerner, the Arab culture and its conventions – based on their rich philosophy, history, language, nomadic heritage and religion – are often confusing, and yet an understanding of them helps greatly to build rewarding relationships. There is probably no better means of coming to terms with the Arab business world than employing a local representative. His knowledge will help not only with language and cultural concerns, but also in the vital decision-making processes.

Power structure

No Arab constitution is more than 80 years old. Most are ruled by a single leader or president. The hierarchy is often from a single tribe, Muslim sect or dynasty which hold tightly to the reins of power. The ruler is supported by a council of ministers and advisers, with the dominating power usually vested in the military.

Decisions

Major business decisions are made at the very highest level, but not necessarily by those with whom one negotiates. Delays are often created by the need to pass every decision uphill for confirmation. But the overlord's omnipotence can sometimes mean surprisingly quick rulings, and fast implementation.

Patience

Despite the sand-planted skyscrapers and the chromium-plated hotels, restaurants and limousines, the pace of life in the Arab world is more that of the graceful *dhow*. Punctuality is not considered a major virtue; appointments are made to give one only a rough guide as to the time of attendance. Tight schedules loosen soon after arrival.

Most Arab bureaucracy is modelled on a European pattern, but with an even more torpid tempo. It is counter-productive to try to browbeat officials in an attempt to speed things up. To attempt bribery – which in some Arab countries may appear quite a widespread practice – is a fool-hardy step for a Westerner. Not only can it demolish credibility and business relationships, but, worse still, it can result in a harsh prison sentence.

'As international trading becomes more and more part of the working life of professional people, it is necessary to understand the customer's culture and to adapt to his or her perception of appropriate etiquette. Good social skills are an essential requirement of successful business communication and are often the difference between gaining or losing a contract.'

BRIAN BLUNDEN, Managing Director of PIRA UK (The research association for the paper and board, and printing and packaging industries).

Dress

Appearance is very important in the Arab world as it reflects one's status. Westerners are expected to wear suits and ties for business. Safari suits are acceptable at informal occasions, long trousers and shirtsleeves for general wear. Women's skirts should reach below the knee (in Saudi Arabia, below the ankle), with blouses covering the elbow. They should not wear trousers. Away from recreational areas, swimwear or shorts should not be worn.

Westerners are expected to respect but not to imitate the Arab way of life. For example, in Oman it is against the law for a non-Arab to wear Arab dress and nowhere is it acceptable for non-Muslim Westerners to carry prayer beads. When entering some houses and buildings, shoes should be removed.

The Arab touch and sole

Arabs are tactile. They consider our reluctance to make body contact cold and aloof. In general they are warm and sociable, sensitive by nature, and with an acute and often teasing sense of humour.

Shaking hands is mandatory and can be more than a ritual. They often maintain their grip on one's hand to establish friendship, and it is ungracious to withdraw. Friends will embrace warmly and kiss cheeks, a custom normally extended to Western friends only after long acquaintance.

None of this relates to women, who must not be touched under any circumstances.

The left hand is normally reserved strictly for personal hygiene and is never used for touching food, drink, cigarettes or people in public.

The sole of the foot should never be pointed towards another person. Even when seated on cushions, the foot should be curled inwards or positioned flat on the floor.

Whistling in public is considered bad manners in some Arab countries.

Meetings

At their best, business meetings in the Arab world are relaxed and friendly affairs. Preliminaries take time, and such issues as price are rarely mentioned until the end, or more likely at a subsequent meeting.

When shown into a meeting room, the visitor will probably be given a seat next to the top man. This should not give him ideas above his station. Newcomers are normally given this privilege, and may have to move aside when the next person arrives.

Business cards should be handed to the principles at the meeting, and should be printed in both languages.

One should maintain complete respect at all times for one's hosts, their organisation and procedures. A display of petulance if one has been kept waiting, or of any other manifestation of impatience, arrogance, criticism or supercilious behaviour of any kind, may be greeted impassively but will be noted and held against the transgressor. Likewise servility and lack of self-esteem.

It is quite possible that people who are total strangers to you may sit in on your meeting, or enter and sit down to observe the proceedings. If it is all right with your host, it should be all right with you.

Before discussing business, a prolonged exchange of pleasantries, and the serving of tea or coffee, are customary.

171

When one gets down to business, some Arab businessmen appear not to be paying much attention to one's presentation. They may look languidly around the room, focus on the middle-distance, fidget, fiddle with their cup or rings and so on. It is their way, and one should not be under the impression that they are not paying attention. Arabs have an enviable ear for detail.

The Western hard sell is neither appreciated nor effective. A friendly approach to business works best. That may take time to build, but the relationships thus established will be valued and valuable to both sides.

Negotiating

The principles of negotiating in the Arab world are seen in many areas of general commerce, so it can be a useful trial run for the businessman to test them out for smaller stakes in a local market – or souk. The art of compromise has been established in the Arab world for centuries. It is based on not losing face: the equivalent, in Western terms, of both sides getting good value and remaining on good terms.

In all business negotiations, time is a weapon; to try to hurry is to put oneself at a disadvantage. One should not feel the need to finalise a deal at the first meeting. Nor should one show that one actually needs what is being sold or traded.

Integrity is the essential quality. In the Arab world one is expected to keep one's word, to the letter, at all times.

Although the atmosphere at business meetings in the Arab world is generally cordial, one should beware of over-familiarity. One should not discuss politics, religion or sex.

Addressing dignitaries

When addressing an Arab one starts with the word 'Ya' meaning 'Oh'. For all the following phrases, place the stress on the underlined syllable. Spellings are phonetic.

- When being introduced to an Arab ambassador address him as *Ya Sa'aadat As-Safeer*, thereafter as *Sa'aadatak*.

- A king – *Ya Jalaalat Al-Malik* on introduction, then *Jalaalatkum*

- A crown prince – *Ya Saahib Assumoo*

- A prince – *Ya Sumoo Al-Ameer*

- An imaam – *Ya Fadeelat Al-Imaam*

- A ruling sheikh – *Ya Samaahat As-Sheikh*
- The President of a country – *Ya Fakhaamat Ar-Ra'ees*
- A Prime Minister – *Ya Dowlat Ar-Ra'ees*
- A government minister – *Ya Mak'aalee Al-Wozeer*
- A company director or manager – *Ya Sa'aadat An'Na'ib* on introduction, then *Ya Mudeer*
- A professor – *Ya Ustaaz*
- An ordinary person (let's call him Mr Gadar) – *Ya Gadar*
- Mrs Gadar – *Ya Madaam*
- Servants or waiter – *Ya Akh*.

> 'Too many British firms still consider it unnecessary to learn the customer's language, customs or business practices, with the result that orders are lost to competitors who have taken the trouble to do so. Indeed, it is suspicious that the only people nowadays who openly say that the UK has a marketing advantage from speaking English are our competitors.'
>
> BRIAN WARD LILLEY, Director General of the Institute of Personnel Management.

Presents

Fine-quality presents may be discreetly presented to Arab businessmen. If they are given to more than one person, then great care should be taken that they are graded according to the seniority of the recipients.

Beware of appearing too anxious to consummate a deal by giving too extravagant a gift.

Receptions

The timing and conduct of receptions is normally as in the West, but with the following differences:

- Usually, no alcohol

173

- Only the right hand is used for eating, drinking, and – most difficult to remember – smoking

- Guests should try to arrive within a few minutes of the stated time of arrival and departure. They will normally be greeted and seen off by the hosts

- Wives may attend by invitation, but they will probably be segregated and other guests' wives should not be addressed by the men without an introduction.

Western businesswomen

Businesswomen have been very successful in the Arab World in recent years, but in some countries they still find their Arab associates ill at ease with them. Many find it essential to employ a local agent or representative to accompany them throughout the business day.

Most older Arabs seem allergic to women who act in either an aggressive or over-flirtatious manner. They prefer Western women to dress soberly and to behave in a polite and respectful manner – which is precisely what they expect from Western men, too.

The business week

In Muslim countries, Friday is the holy day, so no business is conducted. In some Middle Eastern countries businesses are also closed on Sundays. Saturday is a normal working day.

Important dates

The Muslim calendar loses eleven days each year, and is based on physical sighting of the moon, so dates may vary from country to country. The following are the approximate months for important festivals for all Muslims. However do check before making any arrangements, as the exact dates change each year.

- February – one day: Lailat Al-Isra wa Al-Mi'raj (The Prophet's night journey to heaven)

- April – three days: Id Al-Fitr (end of Ramadan)

- June – four days: Id Al-Adha (Pilgrimage to Mecca)

- July – one day: Al Hijra (Islamic New Year)

- September – one day: Milad al-Nabi (The Prophet's Birthday)

- Always the ninth month of the Muslim calendar year: Ramadan – the month of refraining from eating, drinking and smoking between sunrise and sunset. Foreigners should not be seen doing so, either.

Most offices close two days before Id Al-Fitr. Government offices close during the last week of Ramadan.

June to September are peak summer months in most of the Arab world, with temperatures ranging from uncomfortable to unbearable. Most Arab businessmen take long holidays during this period.

The period around the festival of Id Al-Adha is best avoided, as are the last two weeks of Ramadan and the two weeks thereafter, during which many people take another short holiday.

Chapter 24
═══════

RELIGIOUS AND SOCIAL LIFE IN THE ARAB WORLD

THE Arabs are a garrulous and hospitable people who like to receive visitors and make new friends. This may be explained by their origins in the desert, where one's relationships with neighbours were crucial to survival.

Much entertaining goes on at home, often with a large number and variety of guests. This is invariably organised by the women, behind the scenes. They usually go to great pains to organise hospitality for guests, although visiting foreigners are not often privileged to meet them.

Arabs have contributed enormously to world philosophy, literature and mathematics. Today, the Islamic religion and culture is spreading at an extraordinary rate around the world, and will no doubt have a huge influence on the world in future.

Introduction to Islam

Arabs can trace their history to over 3000BC. The word 'Arab' comes from the Semitic word meaning 'desert dweller'. The founder of Islam, Muhammad, was born in Mecca, in what is now Saudi Arabia, around AD571. He was a member of the powerful Quaraysh tribe. At the age of forty he recognised himself as the Prophet and vigorously propagated the religion of Islam. His divine revelations were preserved in the sacred scripture, the Koran (Qur'an). The Koran is believed to contain everything that has happened and will happen in the universe. As God spoke to Muhammad in the Arab tongue, this is considered the holy language. The book is written in a powerful and poetic vernacular, and is the wellspring of Arab eloquence, a quality much admired by peoples of the Arab world.

Millions of Muslims pray to Mecca five times a day, and do so in shops, offices, streets and wherever they happen to be. All determine to make the pilgrimage to the holy city at least once in their lifetime. God's will was revealed to Muhammad at Mecca and Medina. Entry to both these cities is forbidden to non-Muslims.

Some countries allow non-Muslims to enter mosques. Shoes must be removed, and women must wear head-scarves.

Arab women

Many people have an over-simplified and inaccurate view of women in Muslim societies. Although women have become more emancipated in many Arab countries in recent years (particularly in more sophisticated countries like Egypt), Westerners are inclined to regard Arab women as mere male chattels. The women themselves do not think so, nor do their men. Islam unquestionably regards them as equal. Indeed in most families they are much more than equal, with considerable influence over everyone. The mother is considered the axis of movement of Muslim society, with the pivotal role of training future generations.

Nevertheless, in strictly muslim societies like Saudi Arabia, the lives of women may appear to be inhibited. The daily routines in the more orthodox and the less-cosmopolitan classes, are often regulated in the following ways:

- At home, many live in segregated quarters and are prohibited from meeting male – but not female – guests
- Outdoors, they wear full-length black gowns with veils and walk behind their husbands. It is discourteous for a stranger to address them except through their escort
- They are prohibited from driving
- They do not visit friends unless accompanied by a male relative
- The educated classes may go to work, but they are not encouraged to enter professions which bring them into direct contact with men; medicine is one of the few exceptions.

Women are also active in law, commerce – often employing men to handle customer contact – the media, agriculture and light industry. In 1989 a mass-circulation Islamic publication cited Western women as being the oppressed ones. It scorned the notion that they are free and liberated, calling them slaves to offices, factories, clubs, shops and cabarets, and saying that their sexuality was exploited by men. An uncomfortable picture, but probably not a great deal more distorted than our view of Arab women.

The family

Arab families are close-knit, large and usually fiercely loyal to one another. Several generations often live together, headed by the venerated elders.

Islam permits a man to have up to four wives, but insists that all must be treated equally. Women who support the concept of polygamy give as one of their reasons that it offers them more freedom. Divorce is not difficult to obtain in most Arab countries, where even long marriages are ended by a simple ritual. Men are honour-bound to provide financial support throughout their ex-wives' lives.

Attitudes

However shocked we may be at the harshness of Arab law in some countries, in particular the statutory physical punishments in some countries, it is nothing to what many Muslims think of the state of the West. Against their record of generally low crime levels, they read with horror the Western catalogue of hooliganism, violence, alcoholism, drug addiction, sexual permissiveness, breakdown of family life, child abuse, homosexuality in high places, Godlessness, blasphemy and widespread iniquity. No wonder they are astonished at some visitors' bland attempts to advocate the Western lifestyle as more 'civilised' than their own.

Hospitality

The Westerner should be careful not to over-indulge in his Arab host's hospitality. When, after others have threaded their way home, an Arab host insists you continue to partake of his food, drink, conversation and other entertainments, he is probably just being polite. There is no Arab equivalent of 'Haven't you lot got any homes to go to?', so he will consider it a personal obligation to be hospitable for as long as you wish to stay. A foreign visitor should therefore ensure that he is not the last to leave.

The Westerner should beware of fulsomely admiring his host's carpets, ornaments, furniture, transport, or other possessions. He could put the host under an obligation to present them to him.

Basic food and drink

Arab food is generally spicy and pungent; it is also one of the great cuisines of the world. Many Arab businesses open up early and close before mid-afternoon. Lunch is normally the biggest meal of the day, and may not finish until 3pm.

Meat is not a staple part of the daily diet for many Arabs. Beef is not widely available, tender or cheap. Lamb, fowl, fish and game are favoured. The consumption of pig meat is forbidden by the Koran.

Most meals are accompanied by flat, unleavened bread, familiar to us as Greek pitta bread. It is used to accompany food, to split open and contain it, and as an edible food grabber. It is also used as an alternative to the ubiquitous rice on which to ladle stews.

In most Arab countries no alcohol of any kind will be served.

Eating, drinking, smoking or passing food are all done with the right hand. The left hand, as mentioned earlier, is never used to accept food or anything else. Sometimes the setting is a low table surrounded by cushions; leaning on one's left arm is a good aide-memoire to keep its hand dormant.

The last course is thick coffee, medium or very sweet. If one or two cups is sufficient, one jiggles and turns the cup in one's hand as more is offered.

After meals it is customary to wash one's hands, either in the basins circulated by servants or waiters, or in washrooms. In both cases, industrial-sized bottles of eau de cologne are made available and profusely applied.

'Doing business with the Arab World is rewarded not only by material gains, which can be in abundance. It is primarily, and more importantly, rewarded by something which is far more precious and which transcends and outlives the mere act of making money.

'People in the Arab World do not treat others simply as sources of supplies or services, however great their need of such goods and services. They look at them as being worth knowing in their own right and of being capable of receiving, appreciating and giving back friendship. They also expect their visitors to approach them as human beings capable of seeing trade relations as a genuine and rewarding human encounter, not merely as goods for money.'

A K AL-MUDARIS, Secretary-General and Chief Executive of the Arab-British Chamber of Commerce.

Vocabulary

Arabs are delighted when a foreigner makes the effort to speak their language. Mastering it is extremely difficult, but the exchange of a few general phrases will be openly appreciated and mistakes overlooked.

For all the following general words and phrases, place the stress on the underlined syllable. Spellings are phonetic.

- Please = *Minfudluk*

- Thank you = *Shukraan*

- Pleased to meet you = *Tasharrufna*

- Welcome = *Ahlan Wa Sahlan*

- Welcome to you, too = *Ahlan Wa Sahlan Beekum*

- Hello = *Muruhuba*

- Good morning = *Sabaah Al-Khair* (reply *Sabaah An-Noor*)

- Good afternoon = *Masaa Al-Khair* (reply *Masaa An-Noor*)

- Greetings (Peace be with you) = *As-Salaam Alaykum* (reply *Wa Alaykum As-Salaam*)

- Goodbye = *Maa As-Salaama* (reply *Allah Yisullmak*)

- Goodnight = *Tisbah Ala Khair* (reply *Wa Inta Min Ahla*)

- Yes = *Aiwa* or *Na'aam*

- No = *La* but the word is rarely used outright in business – it is one's attitude that indicates a negative response. An Arab businessman may instead use the expression 'Peace be with you' (*Salaamatak*)

- How much? = *Kam?*

- A little = *Qaleel*

- Congratulations = *Mabrook*

- I understand = *Afham*

- I don't understand = *Ma Afham*

- Sorry! = *Muta'assif*

- My name is Fellows = *Ismee* Fellows

- (And if all else fails . . .) Do you speak English? = *Tatakullam Ingleezee?*

Religious terms:

- God is most great = *Allahu Akbar*
- Come to prayer = *Hayy Ala-Al-Salah*
- Pilgrimage (to Mecca) = *Hajj*

182

USEFUL ADDRESSES

Business Etiquette

Business Etiquette Ltd. runs training courses covering essential business culture in the UK, the European Community, Japan, the Middle East and elsewhere. For details please phone (UK): 01306 876601

The Arts

Association for the Business Sponsorship of the Arts (ABSA), 60 Gainsford Street, London SE1 2NY. Tel. 0171–378 8143

Ascot

The Ascot Office, St James's Palace, London SW1A 1BP. Tel. 0171–930 9882

Company information

Companies House, 55 City Road, London EC1Y 1BB. Tel. 0171–253 9393

Lords

Lords Cricket Ground, St John's Wood Road, London NW8 8QN. Tel. 0171–289 1611

Overseas trade

British Overseas Trade Board, King's Gate, 66–74 Victoria St, London SW1E 6SW. Tel. 0171–215 5000

Economist Publications Ltd, Marketing Department (Z1),
15 Regent Street, London SW1Y 4LR. Tel. 0171–493 6711

Japan

Commercial Department, British Embassy, 1 Ichibancho, Chiyoda-
Ku, Tokyo 102, Japan. (03) 265 5511

Exports to Japan Unit, Department of Trade and Industry, King's
Gate, 66–74 Victoria St, London SW1E 6SW. Tel. 0171–215 4962

Japan External Trade Organisation, 6th Floor, Leconfield House,
Curzon Street, London W1Y 8LQ. Tel. 0171–493 7226

Japanese Chamber of Commerce and Industry, Room 495, Second
Floor, Salisbury House, 29 Finsbury Circus, London EC2M 5QQ.
Tel. 0171–628 0069

Japanese Embassy, 101 Piccadilly, London W1V 9FN.
Tel. 0171–465 6500

Middle East

Arab-British Chamber of Commerce, 6 Belgrave Square, London
SW1X 8PH. Tel. 0171–235 4363

Committee for Middle East Trade, Bury House, 33 Bury St,
London SW1Y 6AX. Tel. 0171–839 1170

The Middle East Association, Bury House, 33 Bury St, London
SW1Y 6AX. Tel. 0171–839 2137

The Queen's Awards

The Queen's Awards Office, Bridge Place, 88–89 Eccleston Square,
London SW1V 1PT. Tel. 0171–222 2277

Wimbledon

All England Lawn Tennis Club, Church Road, Wimbledon
SW19 5AE. Tel. 0181–946 2244

Women's Networks

Women in Management, 64 Marryat Road, London SW19 5BN
Tel. 0181–674 1991

Association of Women Solicitors, The Law Society, 114 Chancery Lane, London WC2A 1PL. Tel. 0171–242 1222

Network (for women at the very top in the professions, industry and the arts), PO Box 7706, London SW1P 3XN. Tel. 0171–222 2524

Other valuable organisations, some of which are listed in British Telecom's London *Business Pages*, include: Women in Construction Advisory Group, Women in Engineering, Women's Education in Building, Women in Publishing and Women in Industry.

INDEX

Business Books for Successful Managers

PIATKUS BUSINESS BOOKS have been created for busy executives and managers who need expert knowledge readily available in a clear and easy-to-follow format. Titles include:

The Art of the Hard Sell *Subtle high pressure tactics that really work* Robert L. Shook

The Best Person for the Job *Where to find them and how to keep them* Malcolm Bird

Better Business Writing *How to give extra power and clarity to your memos, letters and reports* Maryann V. Piotrowski

Confident Conversation *How to talk in any business or social situation* Dr Lilliam Glass

Confident Decision Making *How to make the right decision every time* J. Edward Rosso and Paul J. H. Schoemaker

The Complete Time Management System Christian H. Godefroy

Corporate Culture Charles Hampden-Turner

Creative Thinking Michael LeBoeuf

Dealing with Difficult People *How to improve your communication skills in the workplace* Robert Cava

The Energy Factor *How to motivate your workforce* Art McNeil

Guerrilla Marketing Excellence Jay Conrad Levinson

Guerrilla Marketing Jay Conrad Levinson

Guerrilla Marketing On The Internet Jay Conrad Levinson and Charles Rubin

How to Implement Change in Your Company John Spencer and Adrian Pruss

How to Win Customers and Keep Them for Life Michael LeBoeuf

How to Write Letters that Sell Christian Godefroy and Dominique Glocheux

The Influencial Woman *How to achieve success without losing your femininity* Lee Bryce

Life's a Pitch *How to outwit your competitors and make a winning presentation* Don Peppers

For a free brochure with further information on our complete range of business titles, please write to:

Piatkus Books
Freepost 7 (WD 4505)
London W1E 4EZ

PIATKUS

Business Etiquette Training Programmes

Company in-house and open training programmes are held throughout the UK, focusing on:

* First and Lasting Impressions
* Entertaining in Business
* Relationships in the Workplace
* Customer Service and Complaints

Foreign business etiquette and culture training programmes are held for national and international companies. A one-day course includes:

* Understanding the Culture of your Foreign Clients
* Communicating Successfully
* Developing Social Skills
* Appreciating Eating Customs
* Language and Greetings

For further details, please contact:

Business Etiquette Ltd
Studio One C
Chapel Lane
Westcott, Dorking
Surrey RH4 3PJ

Telephone 01306 876601
Fax 01306 875336